THE LOST VILLAGES
OF DORSET

THE LOST VILLAGES
OF DORSET

RONALD GOOD

THE DOVECOTE PRESS

First published as a paperback in 1987 by
The Dovecote Press Ltd
Stanbridge, Wimborne, Dorset
First published in 1979
0 946159 43 2

© Ronald Good 1979, 1987

Printed and bound by Biddles Ltd
Guildford and King's Lynn

Contents

Illustrations

MAPS

N.B. On maps 3 – 18 county roads are shown as a continuous line and old roads and tracks are shown as a broken line.

AERIAL PHOTOGRAPHS

Preface

The aim of this book is to give a brief outline of one particular aspect of Dorset's history, namely the ways in which the rural settlements in the county, and their distribution, have changed during the past thousand years or so. Some villages have vanished, some have become little more than shadows of their former selves, and others, though they may now be as populous as they have ever been except perhaps during the middle decades of the nineteenth century, have nevertheless suffered considerable change of one sort or another. Yet all are of interest, and each adds something to the story.

For this kind of account the ancient county of Dorset, as it was defined in the earliest years of the present century, is remarkably well supplied with basic sources of information. The most valuable, and indeed indispensable, of these is John Hutchins' great book, *The History and Antiquities of the County of Dorset*, which first appeared in two volumes in 1774, shortly after the death of its author. A second edition was published in 1813, and a third edition, of four large volumes edited by W. Shipp and J. W. Hodson, was published between 1861 and 1870. This third edition is the most familiar but, unless otherwise stated, the references in the following pages are to the first edition. A facsimile of Shipp's edition was published in 1973.

'Hutchins', as it is commonly called, has a useful small-scale map of Dorset as a frontispiece, but it was a fortunate coincidence that, in 1765, Isaac Taylor of Ross produced the first map of the county on the now familiar scale of one inch to one mile. This was another immense work, carried out as far as is known by a single individual as part of his professional life as a surveyor, at a time when it could only have been done conveniently on horse-

back. Although Taylor is not to be compared with Hutchins as a piece of scholarship, the two together provide a remarkably useful and complementary historical source.

In recent times too Dorset has been fortunate because it has been thoroughly surveyed and inventoried by the Royal Commission on Historical Monuments (England) and the beautifully illustrated volumes of its report, hereinafter referred to as *RCHM*, are magnificent productions. The first volume, covering a generous West Dorset appeared, after many years in preparation, in 1952, and at that time no particular attention was paid to sites or remains of medieval settlements. This has been remedied in subsequent volumes, namely: II (South-east Dorset) published in 1970; III (Central Dorset), 1970; IV (North Dorset), 1972; V (North-east Dorset), 1975. The frequency of references to these five volumes in the following chapters is sufficient testimony to their outstanding value to all those interested in the history of Dorset.

The *Victoria County History of Dorset*, referred to here as *VCH*, though begun in 1908 has yet to be completed, but it nonetheless includes much of value. The original volume (II) has a long account of the ecclesiastical history of the county, and shorter sections on its political, maritime, social and economic history, and on agriculture and industry. The comparatively slim volume III, edited by R. B. Pugh and published in 1968, is devoted entirely to Domesday Book and the Geld Rolls. It includes translations of both, as well as a map, and is most valuable.

Another very important source of information about almost all aspects of the county's history, is the long series, now of close on one hundred volumes, of the *Proceedings of the Dorset Natural History and Archaeological*

Society, references to which are shown in the notes by the abbreviation Proc., followed by the volume number and date of publication.

It would be invidious to make a long selection from the ever-lengthening list of individual books about Dorset, but as far as the present subject is concerned the following are especially worth consulting: R. W. Eyton, *A Key to Domesday* (Dorset), Dorchester, 1878; A. Fägersten, *Dorset Place Names*, Uppsala, 1933; A. Oswald, *Country Houses of Dorset*, 2nd ed. London, 1959; R. Good, *The Old Roads of Dorset*, 2nd ed., Bournemouth, 1966 (hereinafter referred to as ORD); and C. C. Taylor, *Dorset*, published in 1970 as a part of a series *The Making of the English Landscape*.

In addition to these printed sources there is an immense store of historical material in the Dorset Records Office, Dorchester, and in the library of the Dorset Natural History and Archaeological Society at the County Museum, Dorchester; this latter including the typescript of a short essay on lost Dorset villages by P. W. Lock. The County Library, Dorchester, and Poole Reference Library also have good collections of Dorset literature.

There is still another fund of information which, because of its character, is all too easily overlooked. This is the personal knowledge of those who, whether born in the county or not, have, by long acquaintance with it, acquired a store of fact or tradition which used in the right context can be a great help. Knowledge of the Dorset countryside and its topography enables scenes to be pictured with some reality and aids the recognition and assessment of clues which might otherwise pass unnoticed.

To all these must be added the invaluable maps of the Ordnance Survey, referred to here as OS. The most familiar are the various editions drawn on the scale of one inch to one mile, of which the first, as far as Dorset is concerned, is dated 1811, and the latest 1970–1972. This last, herein called 1 OS is, like its immediate predecessors, over-printed with the National Grid of one kilometre squares, enabling map references to be given with great accuracy. However, this method is not widely familiar, and for this reason map references are, in general, given in what is now regarded

as the old fashioned way by citing the direction and distance from some easily identifiable spot actually shown on the map. This latest edition also, and for the first time, shows the public rights of way in red. On these maps, of which sheets 166, 177, 178 and 179 cover practically the whole of Dorset, all the roads maintained by the County Council are shown in colour and are described in the following pages as 'county roads'. During the last few years a new series of OS maps on the scale of 1/50,000 (about $1\frac{1}{4}$ inches to the mile) have been published, and the 1 OS is no longer readily available, but how soon these will supplant, in popular affection and common use, the old easily understood 'one inch is one mile' remains to be seen.

Less familiar are the OS maps drawn to a scale of six inches to one mile, referred to here as 6 OS. The first edition of these appeared in the 1880s and a second called the 'County' edition, was published for Dorset between 1902 and 1931. These dates make this edition of special importance, for the maps depict the country as it was during the decades before and after the First World War and before the changes brought about by the coming of the motorcar made themselves seriously felt. A new edition of this map is in the course of production.

The sketch-maps in this book (which are Crown Copyright Reserved) are based on the maps just described, and particularly on 1 OS 1970. Each covers an area of special interest to the subject and includes the names of all the places to which more than passing reference is made in the text.

Many people have helped me in one way or another in the preparation of this book and I hope they will accept this general, but warm, expression of my gratitude. I am especially indebted to Mr. G. D. Squibb, Q.C. for his advice and for reading parts of the typescript; to Mr. J. R. Boyden for his untiring and rewarding efforts to provide the aerial photographs; to Mr. C. E. Bowen for allowing me to see the proofs of the fifth *RCHM* volume; to Major J. C. Mansel of Smedmore; to Mrs. Bethell of Frome Whitfield; to Mr. C. J. Bailey for his help in connection with the

Bride Valley; to the late Mr. C. J. Hooper and to Mr. H. A. Birch for information about the Milborne villages; and to Miss M. Holmes, Mr. R. N. R. Peers and Mr. H. F. V. Johnstone. Finally my most grateful thanks are due to Mr. David Burnett for the time and trouble he has devoted to preparing the typescript for publication.

RONALD GOOD

Parkstone and Albury 1974–1979

1

Historical Introduction

The course of human history has often been compared with that of a river in which the current is usually slow but quickens sharply on occasion; which is constantly replenished from its own sources; and which, though normally tranquil, is sometimes lashed by storms which though they may make themselves deeply felt never wholly disrupt it. Such a comparison is particularly apposite when applied to a single country, and the history of England illustrates it well because although its human past has been long and marked at intervals by great upheavals these have always been brief and between them its history has, on the whole, been calm and unhindered. The analogy is also appropriate because it takes into account not only the eventful storms of the past but also that placid and continuous underlying current which, because it is so unobtrusive, is often unappreciated but which is the real stuff of both national and local history.

The long historical continuity of this country is especially apparent to those who live in central southern England. They are surrounded by the evidence of a history which stretches back for thousands of years and of its successive chapters – Stone Age; Bronze Age; Iron Age; Roman; Saxon; and Norman – each of which brought profound changes in the modes of native life and developed its own characteristics on the foundations of what had gone before until, in due season, it made way for its successor. Some of these changes were drastic, but despite them it is abundantly clear that rural life, particularly as expressed in its husbandry, has always gone on with little or no essential change and that sowing and reaping has always been the heart-beat of the people.

This being so it follows that however much more spectacular the tale of the cities and towns of this country may be it is the story of the smaller agricultural communities, the villages, which more accurately illustrates the changes which have, during the thousand years or so since the birth of the kingdom of England and the early days of its documentary history in the ninth and tenth centuries, gradually moulded the countryside and its settlements into the pattern which existed until 1914, a crucial date which marks the compass of this book and after which many immemorial aspects of country life began to disappear.

The Lost Villages of Dorset is an attempt to throw light on some of the less obvious of these changes, namely the ways in which the rural communities of the county have waxed and waned in size and local importance with the passage of the years, and to suggest some of the principal reasons for this. But the subject is difficult to circumscribe, for it involves deciding which of the many lesser rural communities can be rightly regarded as having suffered loss or change on a significant scale and on that account merit discussion here.

The claims of what are properly deserted villages without inhabitants are plain enough; nor do the larger villages present much difficulty because their histories are generally well enough known to make clear any particular loss in the past, apart from the almost invariable sharp falls in population from their peak figures of the mid-nineteenth century referred to at the beginning of Chapter 6. The real problem is with the smaller places, especially with the farmsteads and larger farms, of which there are a great many, and to decide just which of these have diminished in size, status or population or in any combination of these is difficult. It is therefore best to use the purely empirical method of mentioning only those which, for one reason or another, add something relevant and worth-while to the story of Dorset villages as a whole or which give promise of doing so if studied more deeply.

Changes in population afford one of the most obvious means of estimation but, because no reliable figures are available until the first national census of 1801, they should be approached with considerable caution. Prior to 1801 there are only calculations, but even these are enough to indicate beyond much doubt that during the past thousand years the population of Dorset has been almost continuously rising and that the likelihood of any absolute population loss over a protracted period is less than might be expected, except perhaps for the century and a half following the Black Death and, on a smaller scale, after other similar visitations of plague. Various attempts have been made to calculate the population at the time of Domesday Book (1086), and Eyton (loc. cit.) concludes that when he wrote in 1871 the population had increased only five-fold in the interim. Between 1871 and 1911 (the date of the last pre-World War I census) the numbers increased considerably, but even so the figure at the latter date was less than ten times that of Domesday Book. Some people, however, regard this as an under-estimate.

The rural population of Dorset has long been distributed in settlements ranging in size and importance from large compact villages to solitary dwellings, and since it is not always easy to find the right description for any one of these it is simpler to think of them as of three sorts. First, there is the village proper which is the capital settlement of a parish and contains the parish church (which even today retains some links with local government) and which has its own incumbent, though this last criterion has rather fallen by the way since the grouping together of ecclesiastical benefices. At the beginning of this century Dorset contained some 250 such villages, together with a few other places so called by common usage.

Second, and less important, though often little differing from some villages in size and significance, is the kind of settlement to which the name hamlet most properly applies. In former times this word was often used in rela-

tion to the now defunct territorial divisions of the Hundred and the Tithing, but in the early middle ages the larger hamlets often had their own chapels-of-ease and were in fact satellite communities of a mother church, generally called a minster (1). These satellites were often called chapelries and many of them became separate parishes in course of time. Iwerne Minster, for example, was a large village at the time of Domesday Book served by a community of clergy and with chapels at Handley, Hinton St Mary, Margaret Marsh and East Orchard. Other hamlets were of all sorts and sizes, many of them consisting of little more than one or two large farms. Today the difficulty of deciding which places properly deserve the name of hamlet is greater because, following the rise of Nonconformity in the seventeenth century, many of the older and larger hamlets acquired their own dissenting places of worship, and it is to these buildings that the word 'chapel' is now most commonly applied. More recently again new building has tended to blur the outlines of old hamlets so that it is now hard to point to more than a small number of settlements which seem to fulfil the name in its ancient sense, namely as being more or less self-sufficient communities of people, smaller on average than villages and without church benefices of their own. Fortunately there is no need to make a complete list, but simply as illustrations there may be mentioned Cripplestyle, Cowgrove, West Morden, Briantspuddle, East Melbury, Manswood, West Chaldon, Up Sydling, Gromstone, Stalbridge Weston, Caundle Wake, Higher Kingcombe, Lower Kingcombe, Knighton (Yetminster), Loscombe, Broad Oak and Shave Cross. It should be noted that for many of the places now known as villages or hamlets Hutchins uses the term 'vill', a word with several uses, but one which he seems to have applied in a general sense as simply meaning a distinct population centre.

Much better defined is the third kind of settlement, the farmstead, already referred to. This word is used here to mean a large and often rather isolated farm comprising not only the farmhouse and its various buildings but dwellings for at least some of the farm workers, but here again the bounds are difficult to draw. Some of the largest farmsteads are, or have been in the past, little less than hamlets or even villages, but others have never been much more than small farms.

Most Dorset farmsteads are probably less ancient than the villages or hamlets. Many of the Roman villas were a form of farmstead or its contemporary equivalent, and it may be that some of the pre-Roman upland settlements should also be so described (though these sites are usually referred to, rather loosely, as 'villages'), but no Roman villas have survived and it seems unlikely, if only on the grounds of the dangers attending geographical isolation in disturbed times, that any remote farmsteads were established until long after the Roman withdrawal. It is true that some farmsteads, and even parts of some hamlets and villages, stand on or near the sites of Roman buildings and the temptation to regard this as evidence of continuous human occupation since Roman times is strong, but in fact most of the rural Roman sites are distant from more recent settlements and have, apparently, never borne buildings since. Moreover the Romans would naturally have chosen positions of particular amenity, and some of these would have been equally attractive to their successors, perhaps partly because of the bonus of having building materials easily to hand, but this does not necessarily indicate continuity of occupation since Roman days. Dorset was not fully occupied by the Saxons till the seventh century (2) and much must have happened after the breakdown of the Roman administration. One belief is that many of the towns decayed or were plundered whilst the indigenous Celtic population continued to occupy their old rural settlements until they were absorbed into the new pattern of population distribution developed by the Saxons. Dorchester at least seems to suggest this; the town which succeeded *Durnovaria*, though on the Roman precinct, grew up on a quite different plan.

Some of the places mentioned in Domesday Book, including perhaps the granges (outlying farms belonging to religious houses) were probably farmsteads, as for instance Abbots Wootton Farms in Whitchurch Canonicorum, but most others of this class seem to have arisen later, either as outliers of villages or hamlets or by the decay of larger settlements. It is these farmsteads which are the units most closely related to the gradual changes in agricultural practice brought about by enclosure, a subject which impinges so directly on the history of the rural communities of Dorset that a brief outline of it is essential here.

Enclosure, or inclosure as it is sometimes spelt, is the 'taking in' from the uninhabited or uncultivated countryside of areas of suitable soils so that they can be cultivated for the better benefit of growing local communities. This process is a characteristic phase of all pioneer societies and has been going on since man first became an agriculturist. Indeed, the word 'enclosure' derives from the fact that, if only to prevent the incursion of wild animals or the straying of their domestic counterparts, the areas taken in were usually fenced, hedged or otherwise delimited, a task which, when timber was the only readily available material, must have been amongst the most laborious of the countryside.

When the first concentrated or nucleated agricultural settlements became established it was common practice for each community to clear and cultivate enough of the surrounding countryside to meet the food needs of its population and to farm it on what came to be called the 'open-field' system. By this system the land was first divided into two or three larger areas or 'fields' cultivated in some kind of rotation, and these were themselves divided into innumerable small sections or strips, these then being allotted to the inhabitants according to their relative needs and their social status. Just how widespread this system was is a matter of debate, for it depended greatly on the nature of the soils available, but in Dorset and at its peak it probably prevailed over a considerable proportion of the better lands. Apart from the forests the rest of the countryside, especially that surplus to agricultural requirements or where the soil was so poor as to be almost useless, gradually became known as 'waste'. Later much of this was called 'common land' and became adjunct to the open-fields.

In Dorset open-field cultivation perhaps dates back to Saxon times, but it was at its height in the early middle ages. Although in some ways it was equitable it was a wasteful and obstructive method of farming and changes in the system eventually became inevitable. These usually took the form of the taking-over of the open fields, either by the *force majeure* of the local landowner or by the agreement of the tenants, and the dividing of the land into compact and more easily worked farms each composed of a number of its own smaller fields or closes. Nowadays it is believed that this process began earlier than has hitherto been thought, probably even before the Norman Conquest, and certainly there is evidence of it in the thirteenth and fourteenth centuries (*RCHM*). It seems to have gained momentum in succeeding centuries with the development of the wool trade and the Dissolution of the Monasteries, and there was another outburst of it in the seventeenth and eighteenth centuries, triggered off by the necessity to increase the food supply, and this continued until, by the early years of the present century, virtually all open-field farming had ceased. The later enclosures were generally authorized by Acts of Parliament and are therefore often called 'parliamentary' enclosures. It was some of the first of these that gave rise to the phrase 'the disenfranchisement of the peasantry', by taking from them their own personal rights and stakes in the open fields. In later years, when still more agricultural land was needed to feed the fast-growing population, enclosure was more often than not concerned with the common-lands which, until late in the nineteenth century, made up a great deal of the waste.

Throughout the centuries there was also enclosure of the waste on a smaller and often almost individual basis, little groups or even single persons clearing small areas by their own efforts and for their own ends. In medieval times this was called 'assarting', and both then and later its legitimacy was both complicated and questionable but it certainly had the effect of spreading the rural population more widely. Traces of this form of enclosure survived in Dorset, especially on the heathlands, well into the present century, though in later days it usually took the form of what would now be called 'squatting'.

Although some farmsteads developed out of the earlier enclosures, others were built much later, many during the nineteenth century on

land, particularly the chalk uplands, which became open to fresh exploitation through later parliamentary enclosures. These are usually some distance from the river valleys because, by the time they were built, modern methods of water supply had been developed. Though these are not really part of the story of Dorset's lost villages, it is worth calling attention to what must have been a striking parallel between the circumstances in which the Romans often built their villas and the Victorians planned many of their farmsteads.

In addition to the farmsteads the rural population is now distributed in innumerable single smaller farms which differ only because they are worked by the farmer and his family, perhaps with some seasonal help. Some of these may well be all that remain of once larger settlements, but most are modern, chiefly because the lavish use of fertilisers and machinery has brought more and more marginal land into cultivation.

The proportionate distribution of villages, hamlets and farmsteads in Dorset varies almost directly with its geology, which divides the country into three distinctive regions. In the east, and mainly surrounding Poole Harbour, is a large area of Tertiary deposits which are a western extension of those in the New Forest and the Hampshire Basin. West of this is the huge central mass of the chalk, rising gradually to a steep escarpment and having a very thin southern branch which runs east and forms the Purbeck Hills. North-west, west and south of the chalk the rest of the county comprises a complex series of vales with marked relief and composed of a wide variety of Jurassic rocks; these have been called the Border Vales. Chiefly because the soils vary greatly in hardness, weather resistance and water-retaining capacity the county can be divided into a number of natural regions. A map showing these is reproduced on page 5 and this map has been used as the framework for several later chapters.

Over much of the Poole Basin the soils are derived from the Bagshot Sands. These sands are agriculturally inhospitable and it was not until the outbreak of the Second World War that any large proportion of the land was cultivated, and then mainly for forestry. Bordering

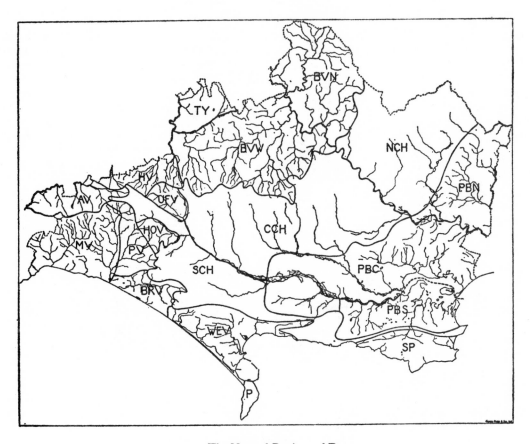

MAP I. The Natural Regions of Dorset

KEY

PBN, PBC, PBS	Poole Basin North, Central and South
NCH, CCH, SCH	Northern, Central and Southern Chalk
BVN, BVW	Blackmoor Vale North, Blackmoor Vale West
TY	Trans-Yeo
UVF	Upper Frome Vales
HV	Halstock Vales
AV	Axe Vales
MV	Marshwood Vales
PV	Powerstock Vales
HOV	Hooke Vales
BRV	Bride Valley
WEV	Wey Vales
P	Portland
SP	South Purbeck

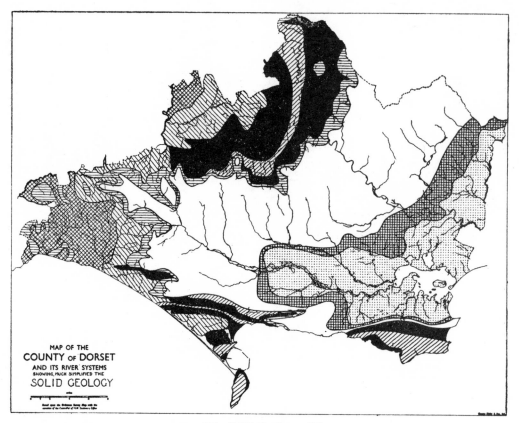

MAP 2. The Solid Geology of Dorset

on the heathland however is a complete but narrow belt of heavier and richer soils of the London Clay and Reading Beds, affording a very different kind of environment which is considerably added to by the wide alluvial valleys of the rivers draining into Poole Harbour.

The chalk and other calcareous deposits provide the arable soils most suitable for open-field farming and it is here that villages are most numerous; but the county has such a complete range of soils that farming of this kind was more widespread than this might suggest, particularly on some of the lighter and less impeded soils with an appreciable calcareous content in the Border Vales. The heavy clays of this part of the county were probably the last to be brought into cultivation and have always been chiefly devoted to dairy farming and stock raising. Here the population is more diffuse because the con-

stant movement of livestock which this kind of husbandry involves is best organised on a rather different pattern of habitation. This is well illustrated in the Marshwood Vales which cover the valley of the Brit and nearly all Dorset west of it. Here, where the soils are nearly all derived from the Lias, some beds of which have a notable calcareous content, there are only a few villages comparable with those on the chalk and other limestones and the bulk of the population is distributed in farmsteads and farms, many of which appear for the first time in documents of the twelfth to fourteenth centuries. These are generally loosely grouped into scattered hamlets but they are never far apart, so that it is often difficult to say where one place-name ends and another begins.

Large nucleated villages are also few in the Poole Basin except on the clay fringe, whence the open fields of the larger settlements often extended on to the adjacent chalk. On the heathlands there was formerly only a thin scatter of population, mainly because the poverty of the soil made it unable to support communities of any size. Today a major influence here is that east Dorset is part of the drier side of England while west Dorset, which has a pronounced relief, is on the border line between the wet and dry sides with a considerable leaning towards the former. Thus the combination of well-drained sandy soils and drier weather has made the east a particularly favourite residential area, with the double consequence that it is now one of the most densely populated parts of the county and that in many parts of it traces of the old settlements have become more than usually obscured.

The general belief is that the villages and hamlets of Dorset date back, by and large, to the centuries before the Norman Conquest and that by the time of Edward the Confessor their numbers and distribution were very much as they are today. For this opinion there is the evidence of a considerable number of late Saxon charters (4) which describe the boundaries of areas which are clearly recognisable parts of, or even wholly coincident with, those of still-existing parishes or other land blocks. Moreover, nearly all the places mentioned in Domesday Book existed in Saxon times and are still known by some version of their original names.

The thousand or so years covered by this book can be divided into many periods, but as far as the history of rural settlements in Dorset is concerned there are four crucial dates. First, 1066, when the Norman Conquest heralded the end of Saxon England and brought with it a new social order. Second, the Black Death of 1348-49, which entered the country through Dorset, took a heavy toll in lives (5) and which brought about an irreversible change in the relationship between landlords and peasantry. Third, the Dissolution of the Monasteries in the reign of Henry VIII, as a result of which most of the great possessions of the Church were impounded and found their way, by gift or purchase, into the hands of prominent members of the laity, so establishing a new class of landowners in contrast to their former ecclesias-

tical possessors. Fourth, at any rate as regards Dorset, was the great outburst of building in stone and brick which seems to have begun in about 1600 (see *RCHM* I p. xxxix) and which, except for the period of the Civil Wars, continued in one form or another for the next 300 years. The beginnings of this period are well illustrated by such houses as Bloxworth, Hanford, Kingston Maurward, Lulworth Castle, Waterston, Poxwell, Wraxall and Wynford Eagle. This fourth stage is clearly different from the others and was undoubtedly an after-effect of the Dissolution, reflecting the gradual percolating down of the redistributed wealth which this had brought about. At all events whilst there are many seventeenth century buildings, both large and small, scattered over the county, especially in the west, there are comparatively few belonging to any earlier date.

It is not easy to give concise names to these successive periods, but it does little harm to accepted usage to call the first the Saxon period; that from the Conquest to the Black Death the early medieval; and that from the Black Death to about 1600 the later medieval. During the centuries since then the two factors which have most altered the rural scene have been the coming of the Turnpike Trusts (in Dorset about 1750) and the establishment of what may be called 'amenity estates'. There had been many great establishments before this, often with hunting parks attached to them, but nearly all these was succeeded by newer country mansions set in their own pleasure grounds from which, largely because of a fear of the proximity of the new turnpikes, the old public thoroughfares were diverted to give a quite new degree of privacy.

That Dorset was, in pre-Conquest times, divided up more or less completely into greater or lesser parcels of land or 'estates' is clear not only from the Saxon charters (6, 7) but more fully from Domesday Book, which gives the names, not only of the new Norman holders but also of their predecessors, a few of whom actually continued their tenure at least as late at 1086. Both before and after the Conquest these lands were held, directly or indirectly, by grace of the king, but just what the conditions of tenure were in Saxon times is not entirely clear. With William the Conqueror and his immediate successors the picture certainly changed, mainly because the Norman kings held the land by conquest and the defence of the country became their first priority. From this necessity there grew up the feudal or manorial system by which the king granted lands to powerful loyal subjects in return for services. Chief among these was the requirement of providing knights and men-at-arms for the king's armies in time of war, but there were also less directly military kinds of obligations, usually determined by local circumstances. The areas so granted by the king came to be called 'manors', each having at its head one or more 'lords' who were responsible for carrying out the services required. These persons became known as 'lords of the manor', a title which is still held by many landowners though it is now little more than honorific. There is an interesting modern account of two Dorset manors, Stratton and Grimstone, by their lord (8). By the time of Domesday Book (9) about one-sixth of the county's rural land was held by the king himself as demesne; some two-fifths was held, as it had been in Saxon times, by the Church; and about half was held by feudal tenants, most of whom were Norman barons. Many details are known about the personalities who held land in Dorset during this period (10).

From the point of view of the lost villages of Dorset the problems concerning the manors, which varied greatly in size especially in the east of the county, is to discover in which of them there was, in earlier times, a lord of the manor with a residence (at first a castle and later a decreasingly fortified manor house) in which he was more or less permanently domiciled; because a dwelling of this style, with all its outbuildings, must have sustained a community large enough to rank as a settlement of hamlet or village size or status. This being so it is not unreasonable to believe that where there are now ruins or more substantial remains of castles or manor houses dating wholly or in part from medieval times, or where such buildings are known to have disappeared entirely, there were once settlements.

All the indications are that in the strictest sense of the word there are no completely lost villages in Dorset, that is to say no considerable settlements which, at any rate since Saxon times, have so entirely disappeared as to have left no material, documentary or traditional evidence of their former existence, a fact which once again stresses the remarkable continuity of local rural life and history. It is true that if there were such places they would, by definition, be unrecognisable and nothing could be said about them; and it is also true that there are some place-names that have not yet been pin-pointed satisfactorily, but that there is no significant number of erstwhile settlements which are known neither by name nor site seems reasonably certain. It should also be remembered that the mention of a name in some old document is seldom enough to identify the place or even to show that it as a human settlement.

From all this it will be clear that all the old places included in the following pages are still recognisable in one way or another, but they differ so much among themselves that the only practical way of dealing with them is to arrange them in five categories.

First and foremost are the old settlements most properly called 'lost' because, although known by name, usually beyond doubt, they can only be identified today by the traces of their deserted sites, nothing or almost nothing remaining above ground. They have no inhabitants in the true sense of the word although in some cases one or two buildings, long subsequent to the date of the original settlement, stand actually within or very close to their sites.

Next, and nearest in kind to the lost villages proper, come those which have almost or wholly disappeared but which have been replaced by large country houses which generally perpetuate their names. It is not always easy to detect how their obliteration came about and whether or not there was deliberate destruction, though an element of this is clear in some cases. The mansions which have supplanted these old villages vary considerably, but in practice they fall into two groups broadly distinguished as major and minor.

After these come the old settlements that survive as farmsteads standing on their old sites and presumably bearing some form of their old names. There are many of these and it is here that the question of population is likely to be most difficult, mainly because in some of them the number of inhabitants today may well be as great as that of the original place, so that the change is really one of status and ownership rather than size.

These three categories do not exhaust the list of Dorset villages to which the word 'lost' can be applied, if only because quite a number of the extant and familiar villages have, over the years, altered profoundly in one way or another so that today they are very different from their medieval forerunners. Indeed this can be said of so many Dorset villages that to mention all

of them here is impossible, but there are certain examples amongst them which illustrate so neatly and vividly the various factors which have gradually led to their partial or total transformation that some account of them must be given.

When these four categories have been distinguished there remains a residue of place-names, mostly of by-gone settlements, of which a name and an approximate position is known. Some of these may be no more than the names of parcels of land, but even so they are worth note because it is always possible that the names are clues to old places and that the study of them may lead to the identification of others.

2

The Milborne Villages

The story of the lost villages of Dorset cannot be better begun than by an account of one particularly notable group of them, namely those situated within the present parish of Milborne St Andrew, about half way between Dorchester and Blandford. The history of these old and closely related settlements is much involved, but it illustrates nearly all the factors and influences, including personal associations, which have brought change, and sometimes disappearance, to rural settlements in Dorset.

The Milborne villages take their first names from the Milborne Brook, which today rises in or near the lake at Milton Abbey (though in earlier times its source may have been nearer the village of Hilton) and flows first for some three miles due south before turning east, and then south again, to join the River Piddle at a point about two miles south of Bere Regis.

The recorded history of the Milbornes begins with the charter by which Athelstan gave land at 'Meleburn' (and in various other parts of Dorset also) to endow his new minster or monastery at Milton (later Milton Abbey). The reputed date of this charter is sometimes given at A.D. 843 but since Athelstan reigned from 925 to 940 this is clearly an error, and modern opinion is inclined to accept the date 939. What happened to this Milborne property during the next hundred and fifty years is unknown but it does not appear as part of the abbey estates in Domesday Book, wherein three parcels of land are called 'Meleburne'. The largest of these, in the possession of Matthew of Moretania, is equated in *VCH* III with the present Milborne St Andrew. A smaller parcel had been held by Odo, the son of Eurebold, since before the Conquest; and a still smaller one had been held similarly by Swain. *VCH* ascribes both these latter to Milborne Stileham.

Just when the different settlements in what were, at the beginning of the present century, the adjoining parishes of Milborne St Andrew and Milborne Stileham achieved their distinctive names is not apparent, but Hutchins, who probably knew the country well because he was once an usher at the school at Milton Abbas, lists no fewer than eight manors and hamlets incorporating the name Milborne, and the first task must be to try and sort these out and interpret them.

The parish now called Milborne St Andrew (see Map 3 and Plate 1) lies immediately south of the parish of Milton Abbas, and the demarcation line between the two has probably long been much as it is today, running roughly east and west at about the level of the parish church of Cheselbourne further to the west. The western boundary between Milborne and Dewlish is likely to have altered considerably, if only because these two villages at one time constituted the Liberty of Dewlish in the Hundred of Whiteway and their historical relationship has always been close.

More important is the eastern boundary, which has certainly suffered change. In the late eighteenth century Milborne St Andrew marched in that direction with Winterborne Whitechurch on the north and with Bere Regis on the south, but subsequently the small parish of Milborne Stileham was carved out of Bere Regis. Thus, when the present century began, the boundary between these two Milbornes ran east from a point on the Milborne Brook about 600 yards north of the A354, and south from the same point along the Brook itself. Since then the parish of Milborne Stileham has been absorbed into that of Milborne St Andrew, so restoring an earlier state of affairs except that what used to be called Milborne

N

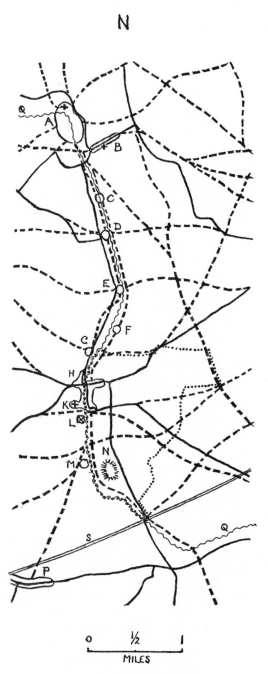

KEY

Existing county roads are shown as a continuous line
Old roads and tracks are shown as a broken line
The dotted line shows the parish of Milborne
    Stileham in 1902

A   Site of the old town of Milton Abbas

B   The present village of Milton Abbas

C   Milton Mill

D   Hewish Farm

E   Bagber Farm

F   Deverel Farm (Milborne Deverel)

G   Cole's Farm and Frogmore

H   The present village of Milborne St Andrew

L   Manor Farm House

M   Site of the deserted village, probably Milborne
    Michaelston, in the Cowleaze

N   Weatherby Castle hill-fort

P   The present village of Tolpuddle

Q   The Milborne Brook

S   The line of the Roman road from Badbury to
    Dorchester

0   ½   1
MILES

MAP 3. The Milborne Villages

Stileham has passed from Bere Regis parish to that of Milborne St Andrew. Thus, at the turn of the century, the village consisted of two parts in different parishes and separated by the Brook. Even at that time the two parts touched and in recent years infilling and new building have fused the two completely.

In his account of the Milborne villages, Hutchins maintains that the original settlement of Milborne St Andrew was not that to which the name is now given; and that the name more properly belongs to the 'tything and hamlet in the N. part of the parish'. He gives no positive proof of this but there is certain evidence in support of it. In his opinion this erstwhile manor and hamlet consisted in his day only of the seat of John Cole and a few cottages, situated 'almost at the north extremity of the parish bordering on Milton Abbas'. His mention of the 'north end of the parish' is unfortunate because there is nothing in the neighbourhood of the Brook that can be called a northern extremity of the parish, and because the old settlement most closely bordering on the parish of Milton is that formerly called Milborne Deverel (or Milborne Cary), now Deverel Farm. But his mention of John Cole identifies the locality more closely.

The Cole family apparently acquired their local property by purchase from earlier holders among whom was the Huntly family, which became possessed of it in about the middle of the sixteenth century and which is described by Hutchins as 'of Milborne St Andrew'. But, as the village now so-called belonged to the Morton family in the sixteenth and seventeenth centuries, it would seem pretty clear that two distinct settlements are here concerned. The most important indication of this is the existence of a thatched building known until quite recently as Cole's Farm, which dates back in part to the seventeenth century. It is not named on 1 OS 1970 but it stands on the west side of the road to Milton Abbas at NGR 825982, a spot which in 1900 was about quarter of a mile beyond the most northerly houses of Milborne St Andrew proper. Referring to this 'seat of Mr. Cole' Hutchins adds that part of it was anciently a chapel, near one end of which bones had been dug up, and that

this chapel was entire and officiated in when 'Mr. King was vicar of Milborne St Andrew'. According to an accompanying list of vicars this name should apparently be Ring, an incumbent who held the living from 1654 to 1679.

Just north of Cole's Farm a lane leaves the Milton road in a north-westerly direction, running for about a mile to West Bagber Copse (a comparatively modern plantation) where it joins the line of the old road from Milborne St Andrew to Ansty and Bulbarrow which, though now but a fragment, is still called Ansty Lane. The lane from the farm is now called Cole's Lane and appears to begin at the Milton road, but is in fact the further stretch of an old highway which came from the east and by-passed the present Milborne on the north.

At this point unfortunately Hutchins becomes confused with another of the Milbornes, Milborne Deverel, and it is best to dispose of this at once. Milborne Deverel is less than half a mile north of Cole's Farm and straddles the Milborne Brook. There is no ambiguity about it because it has been, since before the cartographer Isaac Taylor drew his map of Dorset in 1765, and still is, Deverel Farm. Its second name derives from one Elias Deverel and his wife Christian, whose tenure of it became terminated by death in 1332. Part or all of it seems to have then passed to Thomas Carey, whose surname is sometimes used as an alternative name for it, and in about 1480 it became part of the Morton estates. There are documents relating to it from 1199 onwards, and it seems likely that the Deverels were long associated with it because their name is attached to a considerable area in the extreme north-east of the parish which, until recently was a well-known piece of ancient downland on which stood Deverel Barrow, a noteworthy tumulus excavated in 1824 but now almost destroyed.

Returning to the problem of Milborne St Andrew Hutchins relates not only that it was called Milborne Andrueston, but that the name Milborne Abbatston probably refers to the same place. This last name does not appear in medieval documents but if it is to be taken at its face value it possibly has some sort of connection with the lands granted by Athelstan to Milton Abbey. At all events if Hutchins is correct in identifying 'the seat of Mr. Cole', and if this is now represented by Cole's Farm then the problem is how, when and in what circumstances the name of the present village and parish became Milborne St Andrew.

Many documents relate to Milborne, but the name St Andrew does not become associated with it until comparatively late. The advowson is mentioned in 1254 and in 1263 but without dedication, and according to *VCH* this, presumably to St Andrew, was not made until 1326. Apparently the practice of dedicating churches to saints developed relatively late and was not an essential part of any official procedure.

Meanwhile another name appears in the records, that of Milborne Churchstone or Churchston. It is said that Giles de Bridport, Bishop of Salisbury from 1256, and who consecrated the new cathedral there in 1258, gave the rectorial tithes of Milborne Churchstone to the college of St Nicholas de Vaux in Salisbury, and there can be little doubt that the tithing and manor bearing this name comprised the area round the church. In about 1320 the name appears as Meleburn Churchston St Andrew or simply as Meleburn Churchston, and a little later again as Meleburn Churchston St Andrew. In 1431 the name appears as Milborne St Andrew. It is therefore reasonable to suppose that when the several Milborne manors and settlements were first distinguished by name, the one containing the church, which dates back to Norman times, was called by some form of the name Milborne Churchstone and that later this name gradually gave place to Milborne St Andrew, possibly because the chapel of the original place of that name, which had become disused, was dedicated to that saint. The present parish church is a fine towered building said to have been 'much beautified' in about 1730, and it contains many personal monuments. It also has two fonts, one of them Norman and recovered from the churchyard more than forty years ago. It is perhaps worth noting that although it is commonly understood to be dedicated to

St Andrew, Hutchins does not say so – a very rare omission on his part.

Of the manors and hamlets listed by Hutchins under Milborne St Andrew there remain three, namely Milborne Mamford, Milborne Michaelston and Milborne Symondston. Of the first little or nothing is known, and it may be that the name merely recalls that of a one-time holder whose tenure was so brief as to leave little impact. Milborne Michaelston is puzzling and according to Hutchins its 'site is scarce known', but if it was, as he indicates, on the east side of the Brook it is likely to have been near, or even perhaps an alternative name for, Milborne Deverel. The name occurs in documents between 1320 and 1330. Of Milborne Symondston there are a few records of about the same date, but the family name Symonds (latterly familiar in Dorset) is mentioned only once by Hutchins, and then no earlier than the reign of Henry VIII. Both these latter place-names may also derive from early holders whose tenures were short.

Yet, for two reasons, this seems unlikely. The first is that the village of Milborne St Andrew, west of the Brook, consisted at the beginning of this century of two clusters of buildings with little link between them. The larger one stood on the old road between Winterborne Whitechurch and Dewlish (now part of the A354, and the smaller and more amorphous group included the church and the Manor Farm House. As has been seen there is good reason to believe that the latter is the old Milborne Churchstone, but the other may well have had another name.

The other, and more important, reason is that during the last twenty years or so there has been discovered nearby one of the most notable deserted medieval village sites in Dorset. It lies in a large pasture called the Cowleaze or Culeaze west of Weatherby Castle hill-fort and about half a mile due south of the Manor Farm house. The whole outline, which covers more than 10 acres (and of which *RCHM* gives an excellent account and plan) is plainly visible on the ground. It was probably once served by the old road from Milborne to Tolpuddle, still classified as an unpaved county road, and by the old road from Bere Regis to the Upper Piddle valley, part of which still exists as Snag Lane. Today the Brook runs through part of it because of a diversion about 70 yards westwards in the eighteenth century, a point made more interesting by the fact that for some distance hereabouts the parish boundary with Milborne Stileham was, in 1902, a meandering line on dry land clearly representing the original course of the Brook. There is a remarkable local tradition, long held in the neighbouring village, that a golden coffin is buried in the Culeaze and that attempts to find it bring on storms of thunder and lightning. This, surely, must be a folk-memory of the ancient village.

This deserted village has, uniquely in the county, no known name. It is therefore undocumented, and the question inevitably arises as to whether it may not be either Milborne Mamford, Milborne Michaelston or Milborne Symondston. If so then the likelihood would seem to be that it is Milborne Symondston because Hutchins' brief remarks about it not only suggest that it passed gradually to the Mortons (see below) but includes a reference to Milborne Michaelston which would have been the nearest neighbour of the deserted village.

Whatever the name of the deserted village may have been, there is some circumstantial evidence of how, and roughly when, it became depopulated. The history of what is now the Manor Farm goes back to at least the fifteenth century. The house was probably always surrounded by extensive grounds, including at times a deer park, and by analogy with other Dorset properties this raises two possibilities. On the one hand, if the Manor House estate was laid out during the existence of the old village on the Culeaze the latter would have lost much of its most valuable line of communications with the other. Milborne settlements to the north, and this may well have sounded the death-knell of a village which was perhaps already in decline. On the other hand the laying out of the estate south of the Manor House may have been easier because the old village to the south of it had already disappeared. In either case its demise is likely

to have been in the fourteenth or fifteenth century; a date in accordance both with the complete absence of documentation and building remains above ground, and also with what is known about some of the other deserted medieval villages in Dorset.

It seems possible that even this does not account for all the old settlements in the vicinity. Traces of old cultivation, together with local belief, indicate that there may have been at least one other settlement, at a point about three-quarters of a mile south-west of Milborne St Andrew church.

The parochial vicissitudes of Milborne Stileham (also known as Milborne Bec), on the east of the Brook have already been described but there is one point which helps to make the picture clearer here. In 1902 the village consisted of two distinct parts, scarcely linked by buildings at all. In the south there was a widespread group of buildings, of which the most prominent were Gould's Farm and the farm buildings of Manor Farm. In the north was a more concentrated cluster of buildings along, and chiefly on the north side of, the old east-west road which became part of the Harnham, Blandford and Dorchester turnpike (now the A354) in the mid-eighteenth century.

The establishment of this turnpike greatly enhanced the importance of the villages through which it passed and Milborne became a well-known posting stage through which, before the railways came to Dorset, six main line coaches drove in each direction daily. The village then boasted three large inns, the *Royal Oak* which survives on the north side of the road; the *Cardinal's Hat*, which was slightly further east on the south side; and the *Crown Inn* on the north side of the road east of the Brook. Today the two last have gone and the figure of a white hart stands on a building which may be the descendant of the old *Cardinal's Hat*, but whether, and if so when, there was an inn of the name does not seem to be known. Whether all the buildings on the main road east of the Brook, and thus in Milborne Stileham, were built after the turnpike came is difficult to determine, but it seems likely that there were always one or two there. It may be noted also that settlement remains have been recorded between the A354 and Gould's Farm, but there is no indication of their date.

The Milborne villages had various holders in the early middle ages, but in the reign of Edward IV they became associated with a family which was to dominate their history for several hundred years, and whose heirs, though changed in name by female descent, still live in the neighbourhood. The Dorset branch of the Morton family appears to stem, in about 1400, from a William Morton who, like his son and elder grandson, both of whom were called Richard, are all described in the remarkably detailed pedigree and notes in Hutchins, as 'of Milborne St Andrew'. The most famous member of the family was John, another grandson of William and brother of the second Richard, who eventually became Lord Chancellor, Archbishop of Canterbury and finally Cardinal in the reign of Henry VII (see p. 33). Known to history as the contriver of 'Morton's Fork', John Morton is said to have been born in the parish of Bere Regis in about 1410, and since he later gave the church its magnificent carved roof, it is easy to conclude that the village was his birthplace; but in fact he was born in what is described as 'the antient seat of the family of Morton, then situated in Milborne Stileham, in Bere Regis'. He died in 1500 at the age of 90 of a 'quartan fever', sometimes interpreted as meaning the plague, and left his Dorset property to his nephew John (son of the second Richard above) who himself died in 1527 and is buried at Milborne St Andrew, where there is a monument to him in the church.

The reader may suspect an inconsistency here because Milborne St Andrew and Milborne Stileham were, until comparatively recently, in different parishes. However, there was no church or chapel at Milborne Stileham and Hutchins relates that, in his time, although this place was rated in Bere Regis it buried its dead at Milborne St Andrew in a part of the churchyard allotted to it. This arrangement may have long been in existence and if so it

may be sufficient justification for the phrase 'of Milborne St Andrew'. At all events it seems that in the fifteenth century the Morton family house was in Milborne Stileham and that it was John, the beneficiary of the cardinal (or possibly John's son Thomas who died in 1591) who first built on the west side of the Brook in Milborne St Andrew proper. It seems probable that the new and more westerly house may at first have been but an extension of the 'antient seat' in Milborne Stileham, and that the latter gradually, or after the completion of the new building, was demolished. Settlement remains on the east side of the water support this view, and may also explain why today the dwelling house of the Manor Farm is on one side of the Brook and its farm buildings on the other.

The male line of the Dorset Mortons ended with a daughter Anne, who died in 1723 at the age of 59 having married Edmund Pleydell (who himself died in 1726 aged 75 and is buried at Milborne) and so began the line of Morton-Pleydell. From this there followed four generations of Edmund Morton-Pleydells, the first of whom, born in 1695, began again to rebuild the Manor House in a more prestigious style in about 1730, laying out elaborate water and other gardens, including no doubt the two now-ruined entrance gate pillars west of the house. It is this house (described by Hutchins as being in Milborne Churchstone near the church and on the west side of the Brook) that is the subject of a splendid engraving, made from a painting by William Tomkins, in the first edition of Hutchins.[1]

The second Morton-Pleydell (1724–1794) married Anne Luttrell, and it was he who continued laying out the grounds and erected the obelisk on top of Weatherby Castle. This, now almost hidden in woodland, is mainly of brick and is surmounted by a large copper ball which, having at some time been perforated by shot, has long been the home of honey bees, and until recently bore a plaque with the initials E.M.P. and the date 1761. The third Edmund Morton-Pleydell (1756–1835) married a Richards and had seven daughters but only one son, who died young. It was one of the daughters, Louisa, who married John Mansel of Smedmore, and their son, John Clavell Mansel inherited the Milborne property from his aunt, adding the name Pleydell to his own. This J. C. Mansel-Pleydell was a prominent and much respected figure in the public life of Dorset until his death in 1902.

At this point something more about the local road history becomes relevant and illuminating. The site of the deserted medieval village in the Culeaze covers, or is very close to, the lines of three important old traffic routes. Two of these, namely those from Bere Regis to the upper Piddle valley and from Milborne St Andrew to Tolpuddle have already been mentioned, but the third is even more significant. The old road down the valley of the Milborne Brook from its source at Milton originally ran on the east side of the Brook through Bagber and Milborne Deverel, but by 1765 this had become at least partly obsolete in favour of a road on a drier line west of the Brook. It was this latter road which, after about 1850 when the Hambros bought the Milton Abbey estate, was greatly improved and re-aligned in order to provide a better way from Milton Abbey to the railway station at Moreton. Today both these lines effectively end at the Manor Farm, and there is no continuation, such as might be expected, of either of them down the valley. Instead there is now a county road, bearing the hallmarks of an enclosure road (see ORD) running east of the present village of Milborne and of Weatherby Castle from the present main road (A354) as far as the farm called Ashley Barn. Here older buildings lie on the line of the Roman road between Dorchester and Badbury and the county road crosses the Brook by a bridge which in recent times has replaced the old Roman ford, and continues, by branching to the lower Piddle valley at Briantspuddle and Throop. There can be no doubt that, as far as Ashley Barn, this road *east* of Weatherby is an artificial contrivance replacing an older and more natural one down the *west* side of the hill-fort. This newer road does not seem to be documented but it is not hard to imagine the circumstances in which it came to be made.

The improvements to the grounds of the manor house by the first Edmund Morton-Pleydell included, in the words of Hutchins, 'groves and avenues of trees, pleasant gardens, pieces of water, and everything that can contribute to elegance and convenience', and this work was continued by his successor. Such landscaping and embellishment was characteristic of the eighteenth century, but it often led to closure or diversion of old rights of way. It seems probable that the present county road on the east of the Brook came into being at this time and for this reason.

Several details support this opinion. The old north-south road immediately east of the church at Milborne actually continues for a short distance as part of the present approach road to the Manor Farm. Added to this the main east-west road through the village leading to Dorchester formerly ran through the southern part of the village, and it is on this that the old gate-pillars abut. It is close to this road, too, that the village church, now at the end of a *cul-de-sac*, stands. Moreover the old road between Milborne and Tolpuddle, though it still ranks as an unpaved county road, is now continuous only by virtue of a substitute length on the east side of the Brook in use as an accommodation road for Manor Farm.

Unfortunately, the long story of the Milborne villages ends, as far as is relevant to this book, on a rather sour note. The eighteenth century lake and water gardens of the Manor House needed an adequate supply of water, obtained by making a cut from the Milborne Brook near Gould's Farm. This supplied what survived on 6 OS 1887 as a short stream; a square pond; and a long narrow lake reaching almost to Snag Lane, and traces of these can still be detected. These water gardens at Milborne were laid out about the time that the lake at Milton Abbey was made by Lord Milton, the new owner of the abbey. Both required a substantial proportion of the far from limitless supplies of the Milborne Brook and it was almost unavoidable that, sooner or later, friction would develop between the two landowners concerned. This culminated, in 1796, in a law-suit between the third Edmund

Morton-Pleydell and Lord Milton, who had by then become Earl of Dorchester. The former won his case, but the harm done could not be remedied, and Whatcombe House, north of Winterborne Whitechurch, which had been built about 1750, became the chief seat of the Morton-Pleydell estates. A large part of the Manor House at Milborne was demolished in 1802, but members of the family continued to live in what remained of it for a considerable time, after which it became the residence of the Manor Farm.

3

Deserted Villages

Our knowledge of Dorset's lost villages has greatly increased since the end of the Second World War, thanks largely to the work of the Royal Commission on Historical Monuments, whose recent reports include many plans, map references and other details of interest about them.

The sites of these deserted medieval villages vary considerably amongst themselves, but in the most characteristic there are no remains left above ground and their outlines appear only as shallow banks, mounds and depressions, which in most cases are sufficient to provide a fairly clear picture of their general plans. Vestiges of contemporary buildings remain in one or two, but in others there are now within, or adjacent to their sites, buildings of a later date. These do not seem to be connected with the original settlements, and it is often difficult to say how or when they came into existence. In some cases these more recent buildings are so extensive as to mask much of the older sites.

This chapter includes all the villages of which there are extensive settlement remains, irrespective of whether or not the site is now occupied by later buildings Their most notable feature is that the great majority lie within the boundaries of the chalk, and that of these most are grouped together in certain valleys.
On the Northern Chalk (NCH) are:

KNOWLTON

This deserted village, which lies south of Wimborne St Giles and in the parish of Woodlands, is well known for its ruined church, which lies on the west side of the main Wimborne-Cranborne road (B3078). Knowlton was a Royal manor at the time of Domesday Book and the church stands within a circular earthwork, one of many prominent prehistoric monuments

in the immediate vicinity. *RCHM* V gives an excellent description and detailed plan of the village, showing that it stretched along the south bank of the River Allen for about 400 yards, to the south and south-west of Brockington Farm. There was formerly a fair at Knowlton,[1] later removed to Woodlands. Knowlton Church, which is about 600 yards from the site of the village, dates from the twelfth century, and the fact that it was considerably enlarged in the fifteenth century suggests that there was once a considerable local population. It fell into disuse in about 1650, and was repaired in the early eighteenth century. Shortly after the repairs were completed, the roof fell in, and it has not been used since. One of the smaller prehistoric circles between the church and village has been called 'Old Churchyard', but the significance of the name has not been confirmed. (See map 4)

BROCKINGTON

This large farmstead, still named on 1 OS as Brockington Farm, lies in a small south-eastern extremity of the parish of Gussage All Saints. *RCHM* V shows that the present buildings impinge, on the west, upon the extensive settlement remains of an old village, so that it can scarcely be called truly abandoned (compare Knowlton). These remains cover at least ten acres and *RCHM* V gives a large scale plan of them which includes the deserted site of Knowlton village. The plan is worth study, for it seems to indicate that the two areas may once have been almost or completely joined. Today there is a space of 150 yards between them in which no remains are noted, but any link could have easily been ploughed out or otherwise obliterated and it is perhaps significant that the River Allen runs through the gap. So also does the

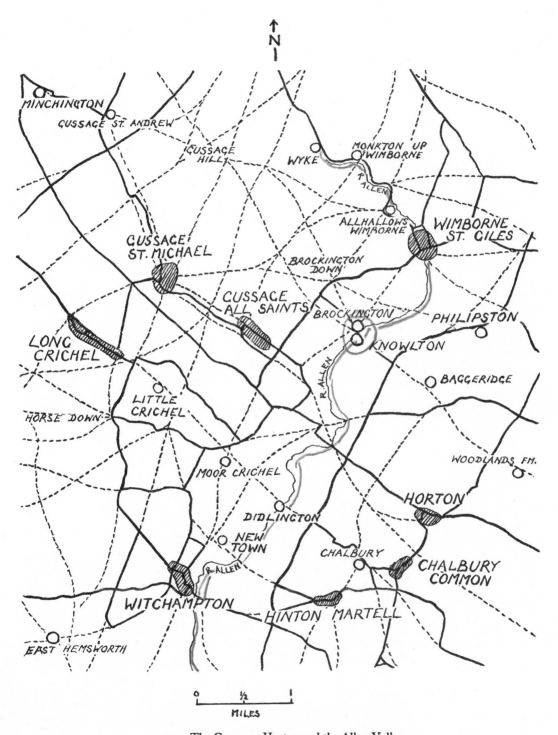

MAP 4. The Gussages, Horton and the Allen Valley

Gussage All Saints/Woodlands parish boundary, but the latter is a comparatively new parish and the boundary looks distinctly artificial. The exact limits of the two villages and the relationship between them, would repay further investigation. (See map 4)

DIDLINGTON

Didlington lies north of Wimborne on the River Allen, just within the parish of Chalbury. Land here was given by King Edred to his minister Wulfric in about 950, and at the time of Domesday it was held by the Church. Hutchins describes it as a 'hamlet ... and here was anciently a chapel', and gives a full description of the remains of the church – including its font, which in 1743 stood in a garden – and refers to foundations, presumably those of the old village. Didlington Farm now stands on part of the site; there are settlement remains to the north-east of the farm, and the name is also used for one of the Crichel Park lodges. By 1765 the village had disappeared, though there was a mill on the River Allen. Since then Crichel Park has been enlarged to the edge of Chalbury parish. Though this enlargement eliminated the old settlement of Moor Crichel, it had no direct effect on the disappearance of Didlington village. (See map 4)

MINCHINGTON

Now a scatter of buildings along the county road between Gussage St Andrew and Farnham, Minchington was once one of two settlements in the west of Sixpenny Handley parish (Gussage St Andrew being the other); and there are settlement remains near where the present road takes two right-angle turns. One or both settlements belonged to Shaftesbury Abbey in the time of Edward II, and the building which in 1902 was called Lower Farm has traditional associations with the church. The extent and size of the old village remains unknown, but because the site is not now occupied by the present buildings it qualifies for inclusion as a deserted village. (See map 4)

PHILIPSTON

This old settlement is included here because its former existence is well substantiated, though its exact location remains uncertain.[2] Hutchins does not place it, but describes it, under Wimborne St Giles, as a hamlet and tithing in the Hundred of Knowlton. It is not shown on Isaac Taylor's map but RCHM V regards it as one of the original settlements in what is now the larger, north-western part of the parish of Wimborne St Giles. It seems probable that the medieval deer park on the slopes of Rye Hill was associated with it,[3] and that it lay near the south-east corner of St Giles Park and a little to the east of the building called Cold Harbour on 6 OS 1902, which was once called Philipston Farm. It must be remembered that the main Wimborne/Cranborne road originally ran across St Giles Park. The road was diverted round the east edge of it in 1787 on a line between Cold Harbour and Rye Hill, and it is quite possible that traces of the old village lie hidden under this diversion. (This Philipston is not to be confused with Winterborne Philipston in the North Winterborne valley. (See map 4)

EAST HEMSWORTH

The name Hemsworth, west of Witchampton, is familiar enough, but it needs explanation. Taylor's map shows two places, Lower Hemsworth and Higher Hemsworth, about 400 yards apart. Today, 1 OS shows both but does not distinguish between them, attaching the name Hemsworth to the large farmstead formerly known as East Hemsworth. Nor does Hutchins resolve the difficulty, because he describes Higher Hemsworth as a hamlet three-and-a-half miles north-east of Shapwick, adding that in the reign of Edward I it was a parish of its own with a market and fair. However, RCHM V includes a detailed plan of the settlement remains which lie between the buildings of Hemsworth and the road between Witchampton and Tarrant Rushton on the north. The remains cover about 15 acres and although some of the present buildings impinge on the site, the main part of the farm does not. It was one of two settlements listed in the Domesday Book, the other, now represented by West Building, being the former West Hemsworth of 6 OS 1902. No medieval settlement remains are recorded from West Hemsworth, but it stands near the site of a Roman villa, excavated in 1905. (See map 4)

Also on the Northern Chalk are two deserted medieval villages in the valley of the little River Iwerne, north-north-west of Blandford.

LAZERTON

This village, which lay between Stourpaine and Iwerne Stepleton, is one of the best-known deserted villages because its site, including that of the church, is authenticated, lying between the present main road and the stream just where the former makes its almost right-angle turn west at the old entrance to the park of Stepleton House. It seems, like so many ancient settlements, to have been a small settlement, with a population of perhaps thirty at the time of Domesday Book, and it had almost disappeared by the middle of the fifteenth century. Its name survives in that of Lazerton Farm, but these farm buildings are so far south as to suggest that they are not within the village precincts. (See map 10)

ASH

The land unit here closely resembled that of Lazerton in size and shape, and lay immediately south of it, but the site of the village is less familiar.[4] Like Lazerton its name survives in that of a farm, Ash Farm, just across the county road (A350) from Lazerton Farm, and which is thought to encroach upon the site of the old village. (See map 10)

The close grouping of deserted villages is most notable on the Central Chalk (CCH). Six have been recognized, within two miles of one another, in the valley of the River Cerne, and a plan of them is given in *RCHM* III, p. 60. Little is known about them and the names of four are by no means definite. All are on the east bank of the river, along what was once the medieval road between Charminster and Cerne Abbas. They are:

PULSTON A

This is in the vicinity of what was called Pulston Farm in the 1930s and is now shown unnamed on 1 OS.

PULSTON B

Close to the first and given its provisional name for the same reason. One of these two is presumably the Pollington described by Hutchins as an ancient manor and hamlet once possessing a chapel.

HERRISON A

Is somewhat nearer Charminster and derives its name from the proximity of the present Herrison Hospital.

HERRISON B

Near the above and named for the same reason. One or other of the two is presumably the Little or North Herringston mentioned by Hutchins, a name derived from the ancient family of Herrings.

COWDEN

The next south and still retains its name. A pair of old thatched cottages stand within its area, but there is no reason to suppose that they are as old as the original settlement.

CHARLTON

Because its site is comparatively large and has long appeared on maps as 'earthworks', it is better known than the others. In about 1350 it was a manor held by the Cifrewast family. The old village is now represented by a northern extension of Charminster on the west bank of the river called Sodern.

Another and even more noteworthy group of deserted villages lie south of Piddlehinton, in the upper Piddle valley near Piddlehinton military camp.[5] From north to south they are:

COOMBE DEVEREL

The site of the village is just east of the stream.

LITTLE PIDDLE

South of Coombe Deverel, but on the west side of the river.

NORTH LOUVARD

Next south, on the east side of the stream.

SOUTH LOUVARD

Once lay opposite, on the west bank of the river.

Of these four villages, three are now deserted and it is difficult to trace their outline, but the name Little Piddle is well-known as that of a hill and a bottom, and the site of the old village and that of Coombe Deverel has long appeared on OS maps as 'British Settlement' or as 'earthworks'. Today, a late-seventeenth century farm stands within the area. Hutchins, quoting Coker, writes: 'Here was anciently a seat of the Deverels, men of no mean antiquity. Now both the name and the place are subverted and scarce the ruins can be discovered.'

A third group of old villages lie between Winterborne Whitechurch and Winterborne Houghton in the upper North Winterborne valley, but of these only three are wholly deserted.

LA LEE

The village stood on the east side of the stream, south of what is now Lower Whatcombe; it is sometimes called Winterborne La Lee. There are only traces of the deserted settlement, but its name survives in that of a large farmstead, almost a hamlet, about half-a-mile to the west. This dates back to at least the seventeenth century, but whether there was a migration to it from the old village or a considerable lapse of time between the two is not known.

WINTERBORNE NICHOLSTON or NICHOLASTON

The site has been recognized and recorded, it lay south of Winterborne Clenston (see page 62).

WINTERBORNE PHILIPSTON

The village lay to the north of Winterborne Clenston and, like the others, seems to have been deserted in the fifteenth century. There is a good account of all three villages, with plans, in *RCHM* III, pp. xlv and 296.

Elsewhere on the Central Chalk there are several more or less isolated deserted medieval villages.

ELSTON

This name has been given to a site on the east bank of Sydling Water, between Sydling St Nicholas and Up Sydling, and is shown on OS maps as 'British Settlement' or 'earthworks'.[6] There are farm buildings called New Barn, close to, if not actually on, the site. It is unusual in being close to two prehistoric hill settlements.

BARDOLFESTON

This is one of the most familiar of deserted Dorset villages, both because of its site and because its name has long appeared, in various guises, on OS maps. It lies on the north side of River Piddle, almost opposite Athelhampton, and was formerly in a parish of its own, held at one time by the Prior of Christchurch Twynham. In the early fourteenth century it had only seven taxpayers and is thought to have been finally abandoned in the sixteenth century, perhaps partly as a result of the building of Athelhampton House in 1495. It is said to have once had a church, on a site known as Church Knap, and the outlines, which cover 15 acres, are still exceptionally clear. *RCHM* III gives an aerial photograph and a plan.

CHESELBOURNE FORD or LITTLE CHESELBOURNE

This village is described by Hutchins, under Puddletown, as 'a tything, anciently a manor and hamlet, long since depopulated, lies near Divelish (Dewlish)'. It was a little north of the old lodge of Dewlish House on the drive that left the main road (A354) a little west of Friar's Bridge at the foot of Bassan Hill. The remains are described as consisting of a series of closes on the west side of the Devil's Brook, but other information suggests that it was always small; with six inhabitants at the time of Domesday, four in 1327, and none by the mid-seventeenth century. This seems straightforward enough but it is at least curious that the name Cheselbourne Water is still applied to the ford over the Devil's Brook near where the old Milton Abbas/Dorchester road crossed the road between Puddletown and Bingham's Melcombe, a spot $2\frac{1}{2}$ miles from Cheselbourne itself, considerably less from Dewlish, and in a different parish from either. Perhaps it is a relic of another lost village which has not been identified. (See map 8)

MILBORNE

The Milborne villages (Chapter II) include the fine site of a deserted village in the Cowleaze or Culeaze. (See map 3)

On the Southern Chalk (SCH) all but one of the five deserted villages are in the valley of the South Winterborne river.

REW

Rew (called Orchard in P. W. Lock's essay) lay midway between Winterbourne Steepleton and Martinstown, just where the words Rew Manor appear on 1 OS. It stood on the old road on the north bank of the river. (See map 5)

WINTERBORNE HERRINGSTON

This is still a parish and is well-known for its fourteenth-century manor house. Hutchins deals with it under Winterborne Farringdon. The seat of the Williams family was then the only building, and it contained a chapel in which the rector officiated since his own church 'went into decay'. No ancient village site has been discovered, but the house was enlarged in 1803 and any remains may be hidden. (See map 5)

WINTERBORNE FARRINGDON

The deserted village lies due south of Dorchester and a small part of one wall of the church may still be seen, standing forlornly in the middle of a field. It is surrounded by extensive settlement remains, of which *RCHM* III gives a plan, showing it to be in two parts; but it is not quite clear whether both of these represent Winterborne Farringdon or whether the smaller eastern part, lying between Chapel Hill Coppice and Home Wood, is part of the old village of Winterborne Came (see page 37).[7] (See map 5)

CRIPTON

Hutchins describes Cripton as 'anciently a manor and vill now reduced to a small farmhouse'; while Taylor's map or 1765 gives the name to a strip of land running south to a small building which is probably the farm mentioned by Hutchins, later known as Cripton Barn. *RCHM* places the old village on or very near the site of what is now called Came Home Farm, but no settlement remains have been recorded

here. Neither this farm nor the old Came Rectory appear on Taylor's map, but both do so on the 1 OS of 1811. This is probably due to the late-eighteenth century construction of the Dorchester and Wool turnpike road. This led to many local road changes; the road over Came Ford was absorbed into the turnpike and it seems certain that the old Rectory and Came Home Farm were built alongside it at some time between 1765 and 1811. If the *RCHM* site attribution is correct (in which case the old Cripton, unlike its neighbours to the west, was on the north side of the stream) it is likely that when the original settlement was abandoned the land associated with it became part of Cripton Farm. (See map 5)

GATEMERSTON

According to Hutchins this was once a 'hamlet which from the blackness of the stones seems to have been destroyed by fire'. *RCHM* II accepts it as a deserted medieval village site and distinguishes it from Lulworth St Andrew. 6 OS 1902 shows the word Gatemerston written across several fields well to the east of St Andrew's Farm. An old road between West and East Lulworth passed through the area, and it seems likely that the old village lay on this road, though the exact site is no longer precisely known.

All the villages so far mentioned in this chapter lie within the chalk or along the adjoining river valleys. There are few other deserted sites, and, with one exception, all are in the south of the county.

HOLWORTH

The site has been carefully excavated and a detailed account of the work has been published.[8] The excavations suggest that the settlement originated in Saxon times, and was depopulated by the end of the fifteenth century. The village has one or two curious features. To begin with there are traces of Roman and pre-Roman occupation within or close to the site. Next, the actual area, now called Chaldon Meadow, fills a small obtrusion in the former parish of West Chaldon, long ago united with that of Chaldon Herring. Holworth appears in Domesday Book as part of the Milton Abbey estates, having been part of

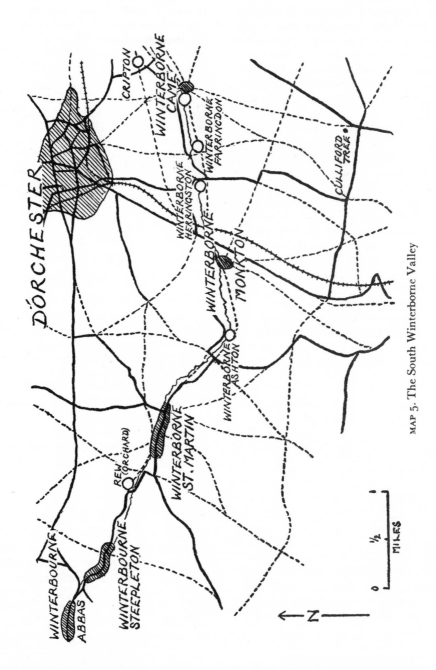

MAP 5. The South Winterborne Valley

King Athelstan's original grant to the foundation. At the Dissolution it passed to Sir John
Tregonwell, remaining a detached part of Milton Abbey parish until 1880, when it was united
with Owermoigne, where, for convenience, it
had long buried its dead. Before the amalgam-
ation it consisted of three tithings in Winfrith
Hundred, namely West, East and South Holworth. The first two of these appear on 1 OS as
Holworth. This does not take into account Chaldon Meadow, the site of the deserted village,
and its peculiar status as part of the parish of
Chaldon Herring may mean that it was never
part of the Domesday Holworth. If so, its history
may be quite distinct and the village may have
once had a different name. The excavated site
lies on a saddle between two shallow valleys,
that on the west running down to West Holworth (Holworth Dairy) and that on the east towards West Chaldon. The geology too is unusual, the area covered by the deserted village
consisting, from north to south, of Chalk, Gault
and Upper Greensand in three parallel and
equal bands. Finally, it must be added that the
deserted village stood on the line of the old road
from the Chaldon valley leading by one branch
to Weymouth and by another to Dorchester.
(See map 9)

WEST RINGSTEAD

The village lies on the edge of the shore at
Ringstead Bay, two miles south-west of Holworth, and is known to many because the outlines of the old village are still clear, covering
about ten acres, and because there still stands
on the site a building said to embody part
of the church. It would seem, from various
sources, that there were once three Ringsteads,
West, Middle and East, more or less side by
side, and yet another further north near Upton.
Ringstead was a parish of its own until it was
united with Osmington, apparently before the
Dissolution, and a church is mentioned as early
as 1224. (See map 9)

WEST BURTON

The first reference to the village is dated 1278,
it was named in the Bindon Abbey Charter of
1313, and appears to have become deserted

between the fourteenth and sixteenth centuries.
It was probably a satellite of the existing village of East Burton in the parish of Wool. It
lies about 200 yards east of West Burton Dairy
on 1 OS in the parish of Winfrith Newburgh.
(See map 9)

MODBURY

The village is one of the two truly deserted
medieval villages in the Bride valley, and 6 OS
1903 places it across the county road between
Litton Cheney and Burton Bradstock at a point
about 1000 yards west of Berwick. During recent pipe-laying operations twelfth century pottery remains were uncovered beneath an un-
stratified layer of alluvial material three feet
thick.[9] Modbury gave its name to a Hundred
and the place-name Chaldecote is associated
with it (but see page 56). (See map 14)

STURTHILL

In Hutchins's day what he called Higher Sturthill was a tithing of Shipton Gorge comprising
Higher Sturthill itself (now only a farm on 1
OS) and Lower Sturthill or 'the chapelry of St
Luke', which is almost a mile further south and
now part of the parish of Burton Bradstock.[10]
The medieval village stood close to the chapel
and its plan, revealed by recent ploughing, fits
in well with the existing footpaths and bridle-
ways. The chapel, which must not be confused
with that west of Ashley, also in the Bride valley (see page 50), ceased to be used in the seventeenth century and was soon in ruins. (See
map 14)

COLBER

This is apparently the only truly deserted village site north of the Chalk in Dorset. It lies
west of the River Stour, opposite Sturminster
Newton, a little south of Stalbridge Lane and
not far south of Colber Crib House on the old
Somerset and Dorset Railway (400 yards north
of pt. 160 on 1 OS 1970). It was said to have
covered eight acres, was a royal manor at the
time of Domesday and Hutchins described it as
'now only a parcel of ground which still retains
the name'. It is thought to have been abandoned toward the end of the fourteenth century, but a field still bears the name. An old

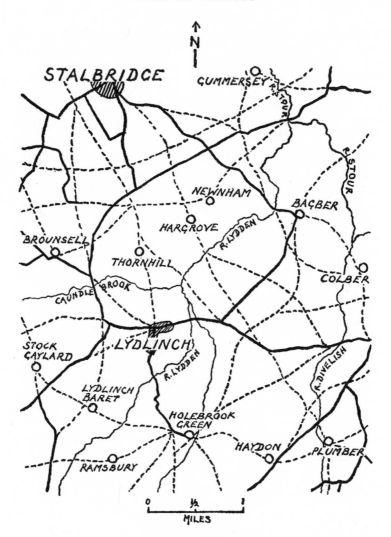

MAP 6. South of Stalbridge

road, now represented by a public footpath from Sturminster which crosses the river by an iron footbridge, passed through or close to the site. (See map 6)

Apart from the medieval villages proper, mention must be made of the surviving evidence of a number of medieval houses whose size suggests that in their heyday they supported populations comparable with those of many of the villages already mentioned. Amongst the most noteworthy are:

ANKETIL'S PLACE

This stood just outside Shaftesbury on the east side of the Sturminster Newton road and near St James's Church. It is said to have been the seat of the Anketils since the reign of Edward I, when a member of the family represented Shaftesbury in Parliament. It was eventually bought by John Still, Bishop of Bath and Wells at the beginning of the seventeenth century, and was demolished in 1790.

KING'S COURT PALACE

The prominent grass-covered site is in the parish of Motcombe, east of Gillingham. It was built by King John in 1199, as a hunting lodge, and demolished by Edward III in 1369. The size of the remaining earthworks indicate that, during its short existence, it may have sheltered a considerable population.

CRANBORNE CASTLE

This is sufficiently apart from the village to make it seem likely that the two had independent origins. It is recorded in *RCHM*, with a plan, as having a motte and baily. Hutchins suggests that it was a Saxon castle and relates how one of the Tregonwells buried a favourite hunter on the motte and then raised a chalk tumulus over the grave.

EAST HEWSTOCK

Today this is known only by the inclusion of its site, including a chapel, as an antiquity, on 6 OS 1904 at a point about 800 yards west-north-west of the first milestone out of Beaminster on the Crewkerne road; but Hewstock is repeatedly mentioned in a long and detailed pedigree of the Strode family given by Hutchins, from which it appears that a William de la Strode came over with William I. The pedigree spans twenty-five generations and the accompanying notes refer to many places still extant and recognizable in the Broadwindsor area. It is first mentioned as West Hewstock in the reign of Henry II. Hugh de Strode lived at Hewstock in the reign of Richard II and the name East Hewstock appears in the next generation. The Strode family became extinct in 1764. Sir John Strode, in a family history of 1628, wrote that 'of the mansion at Hewstock all has disappeared save the foundations of the buildings and portions of the ancient moat'.[11]

NEWTON CASTLE

This is a most remarkable site on a bluff of Corallian rock on the opposite, south, side of the Stour from Sturminster Newton and is the origin of the second part of the name. It is generally believed to have been a medieval castle destroyed during the Wars of the Roses, and is actually situated within the earthworks of a pre-Roman hill-fort. All traces of the castle have disappeared, but the site still contains the ruins of a house, said to have been built in 1544 by or for Queen Catherine (later Henry VIII's widow).[12] The local situation suggests that there must have once been an attendant settlement through which the castle approach ran. It is still reached by a track passing some old houses, but there is no reason to believe that they are surviving parts of the old settlement.

MIDDLEMARSH and GRANGE

These two places, which are so closely associated that they must be taken together, lie in the northern part of the parish of Minterne Magna (itself once part of Cerne Abbas), which now stretches northward across the chalk scarp to the parish of Holnest in the Blackmore Vale. The name Middlemarsh probably first applied to an area of waste ground, but it is now one of the largest wooded areas in the Blackmore Vale. The name Grange, which must not be confused with the Granges north of Wimborne and south of Wareham, derives its existence from before the Dissolution as a farm or grange belonging to Cerne Abbey and was used by the Abbot as a 'retiring place'. Grange now takes its name from a large manor house, perhaps the direct successor of that of the abbot, which was built in about 1600 by Sir Robert Napier. Isaac Taylor's map calls the house Grange Court and Hutchins gives a long account of the building. Eventually, the house passed to Humphrey Sturt of Crichel and, at some point between 1765 and 1870, it was completely demolished, the materials being used for farm buildings. Neither Middlemarsh or Grange appear on Speed's map of 1607, but Hutchins describes the former as anciently a little hamlet and manor 2½ miles north-east of Minterne. It is now a long straggle of buildings on the Old Sherborne Road between milestones 11 and 12 from Dorchester. This part of the road became a turnpike in about 1752 and, except for two farms, the buildings appear to be subsequent to this. 6 OS 1903 shows the site of Middlemarsh Grange (Isaac Taylor's Grange Court) as in a field 400 yards due east of the inn on the main road. The name Grange is perpetuated by that of a farm near the site, on the road between Lyon's Gate and Glanville's Wootton. It seems possible that the old settlement was in the vicinity of the ancient grange and later manor house, and that when the latter was destroyed the population moved to and along the turnpike. The whole neighbourhood, including Hermitage to the west, is of great historic interest and would repay further study. One curious point; about 50 acres of the wood between Middlemarsh and Hermitage constituted, until the beginning of this century, a tiny uninhabited parish called Gorewood.

4

Villages now Represented by Country Houses

MILTON ABBAS

This is an outstanding example of what has frequently been described as deliberate destruction of an ancient settlement by an overbearing eighteenth century landlord. [1, 2] Its recorded history begins in the middle of the tenth century with the foundation by King Athelstan of a monastery or minster, said to have been built near the spot where St Catherine's Chapel now stands. Before the century ended it was refounded as a Benedictine abbey by King Edgar in the valley below. Around it there grew up, first a village and then a small market town which, by the date of the Domesday Survey, was one of the largest towns in Dorset. It continued to flourish throughout the Middle Ages, and in due course a free school or grammar school was founded according to Hutchins by a priest named Sir John Loder, and endowed by the last Abbot of Milton with the estate of Little Mayne (see below). After the Dissolution of the Monasteries abbey and town passed to Sir John Tregonwell. In 1752 it was sold to Joseph Damer, later Lord Milton and eventually Earl of Dorchester, who demolished the Tregonwells' house, replacing it with the present mansion, which incorporates part of the old abbey building. In order to lay out a rural estate he began purchasing leases and holdings as they fell in and, after long and bitter resistance, succeeded in demolishing the old town. Only the school was saved, eventually moving to Blandford in the 1780s. By then Lord Milton had built a new village in a steep valley to the south-east of his new mansion to house the residue of the town population. The almshouse founded by the Tregonwells was re-erected and a church built. Records of the old

town are few, but an estate plan made for Damer at the time of his purchase still exists.

Lord Milton's actions remain controversial. Some believe that the old town was in an advanced state of decay when he purchased it; and the fact that he was able to accomplish his purpose lends some weight to this view. But the majority regard it as a deplorable and reprehensible action resulting in the destruction of a thriving community. The new model village contained forty dwelling houses, each designed to hold two families. At first the new houses were badly overcrowded, and it seems possible that they may have initially housed a population comparable with that of the old town.

There is one further point. The old town lay on the London/Dorchester road, but when the new Salisbury/Dorchester turnpike was planned it was made to run through Milborne, not Milton. The construction of the new road started the year after Damer bought the property, but the plans must have been known well in advance. Ostensibly the new route was chosen because it was less hilly, but bearing in mind the undulations of other Dorset turnpikes (*e.g.* that between Bridport and Lyme Regis), it seems possible that Damer may have been partly responsible for diverting the new road from Milton.

BRYANSTON

Few existing Dorset parishes can have seen so many changes as Bryanston, which adjoins Blandford on the west side. One reason for this is that the parish is divided into two unequal parts; the larger of which lies on the chalk upland, the smaller comprising a length of the flood-plain of the River Stour. The second reason is that the boundary between the two parts is a low scarp, long known at its southern end as The Cliff. The view from the scarp takes in both the river and the town of Blandford, as well as the distant hills, and Bryanston's scenic potential has proved a major factor in determining its history.

In Domesday Book it is not distinguished from Blandford. But by the fourteenth century it had grown into a large village, owing its name to a thirteenth-century baron named Brian de Lisle. The only tangible evidence of its early history is a mutilated stone thought to date from the reign of Henry III and which is now in the Old Church. This little building has been so modernized that its age is often forgotten, but in its present state it is a Georgian building standing at the north end of The Cliff, three-quarters of a mile north-west of Blandford Bridge. It seems reasonable to assume that the old village stood close by, but although it did not entirely disappear until the eighteenth century no remains are now visible.

At the start of the fifteenth century the property passed to the well-known Dorset family of Rogers, and it remained in their hands until it was sold to Sir William Portman in the mid-seventeenth century. After his death the estate was inherited by Henry Seymour, who then changed his surname to Portman. It was Henry Portman who first turned the house and land into a fashionable eighteenth-century estate. The old Rogers house had stood close to the church on the old Blandford/Durweston road. It was now enlarged, the roads closed or diverted, and the grounds landscaped. An engraving dated 1707 shows extensive formal gardens running between the house and river. In about 1780 a new house, designed by James Wyatt, was built on or near the site of its predecessor. Of this house only the stables survive.

No one can be sure whether the buildings in the village were destroyed or merely became redundant. In Hutchins' time the 'vill' of Bryanston consisted of about ten houses on the north side of the London/Dorchester turnpike road, just west of Blandford Bridge and within the parish of Bryanston. All but one of these houses were destroyed in the great fire of Blandford in 1731; but they were later rebuilt and still stand. In this position they are, in effect, an addi-

tion to the present village of Blandford St Mary, and it seems unlikely that they were designed to house the dispossessed villagers of the old village of Bryanston. Taylor's map of 1765 does not show old Bryanston, so its population must have dispersed well before the map was drawn.

In 1890 the 2nd Lord Portman, in a fine gesture of late-Victorian opulence, built a new mansion, designed by Norman Shaw, on higher ground to the north-west of Wyatt's house; which was then demolished and replaced by a church. This latter was clearly intended for a large estate population; but the graveyard at the old church continued to be used for the burial of members of the Portman family. After the First World War Shaw's mansion became the home of a new public school. Although the new buildings constructed to the south of the school now perhaps best deserve the name Bryanston, they have no connexion with the site of the ancient village. (See map 10)

CHARBOROUGH

This was described by Hutchins as 'once a manor and hamlet, now extinguished and depopulated, consisting only of the seat of Mr. Drax and a farmhouse. Foundations of houses have been dug up on the south side of the church, where the ancient vill probably stood'. Only the house is shown on Taylor's map.

The manor was held by Earl Harold prior to the Norman Conquest. By the middle of the sixteenth century it belonged to the family of Erle. It seems probable that a new house was then built, obscuring once and for all any traces of the old village. During the Civil Wars the house was burnt down by the Royalists, but was afterwards rebuilt using some materials taken from Corfe Castle; which the Parliamentarian Sir Walter Erle had helped to reduce. In the middle of the eighteenth century an Erle married a Drax, and – thanks to later inheritances – the family name is now, in full, Plunket-Ernle-Erle-Drax. Oswald states that Charborough has never changed hands through sale, though it has repeatedly passed through the female line.

EASTBURY

The more accurate name for this village, now totally destroyed, is Gunvil Eastbury; and it may be supposed that it was the original settlement of the present Tarrant Gunville, which lies to the north of its site. It stood on both banks of the Tarrant stream close to the present entrance to Eastbury House, and was presumably destroyed when the gateway was built. Eastbury House was amongst the most splendid of eighteenth-century buildings. Designed by Vanbrugh for George Bubb Doddington (later Lord Melcombe), it seems to have been as remarkable as its owner. Unfortunately its size made it impossible to find an occupier after his death in 1762 and, although only completed in 1738, all but one stable wing and the gatehouse were demolished in 1795. The full design of the house is illustrated in Campbell's *Vitruvius Britannicus*, Volume III and the plan is reproduced in *RCHM* IV. Some years later the surviving wing was bought by the famous Dorset Master of Foxhounds J. J. Farquharson to house part of his hunting establishment. When both horses and hounds were sold in 1858 the wing was converted into a country house, the size of which remains eloquent testimony to the vastness of the original building.

EAST LULWORTH

In his *Itinerary* John Leland states that 'the goodly maner place of the Newborows, Lords of East Lulleworth, is hard by the paroch-church'. There is no doubt that the old village also stood here, for although church and village are now separated by parkland, Taylor's map shows the village standing adjacent to the church and castle and it seems certain that most of the old village was eventually demolished and the houses rebuilt to the east so as to enlarge the park. Leland's 'maner place' was succeeded by Lulworth Castle, built by Lord Bindon in about 1600, perhaps employing materials from an older house and from the ruins of Bindon Abbey. In 1641 the property was bought by Humphrey Weld, in whose family it has since remained. Hutchins was delighted by its situation, concluding that 'the only thing it wants is water'; meaning by this that there was no ornamental lake or aquatic garden, both of them fashionable, to set it off. Ironically, the house was gutted by fire in 1929; largely

because there was not enough water available to control the blaze. (See map 15)

MELBURY SAMPFORD

This is the name of a parish in the centre of what is not only the most splendid country estate in Dorset but also one of the oldest, the park at least having been in existence for hundreds of years. It is one of several Melburys mentioned in Domesday Book, and the church, of which the list of incumbents goes back to 1297, was built in the fifteenth century, probably during the lifetime of William Bruning or Browning to whom the estate had descended from the days of Edward III. He sold the reversion of the property to the Strangways family, who still hold it. There is no village now round the church and its disappearance seems likely to date from the rebuilding of Melbury House by Sir Giles Strangways early in the sixteenth century. (See map 7)

MOOR CRICHEL

The history of this parish, some five miles north of Wimborne, goes back to beyond the Domesday Survey and originally consisted of two manors, each with its own settlement; Little Crichel to the north and Moor (or More) Crichel, or Crichel Magna, in the south. In the early seventeenth century it came into the possession of Sir Nathaniel Napier, a member of an old Scottish family which had settled in Dorset during the reign of Henry VII. In 1717 the estate passed by marriage to the Sturts of Horton and was eventually inherited by Humphrey Sturt, Member of Parliament for Dorset from 1754 until his death in 1786. A century later one of his heirs was created Lord Alington.

The Napier house at Crichel, built in about 1650, was burnt down in 1742, but soon rebuilt in 'greater splendour'. When Humphrey Sturt inherited he at once made plans for enlarging the house and for laying out the surrounding grounds. This involved the destruction of the old village, except for the church, which was made a feature of the new landscape. The third edition of Hutchins refers to one rather curious aspect of this:

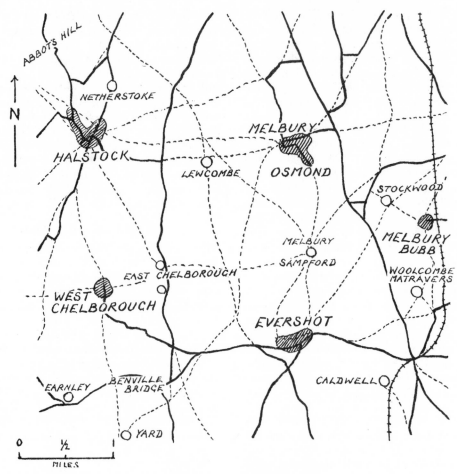

MAP 7. Halstock and the Melburys

There was once a commodious parsonage house in the parish but from it unfortunately standing in the way of the improvements of Mr. Humphrey Sturt, soon after he came to the Napier estate he pulled it down and floated the whole site of it into a lake. He afterwards consolidated the rectory with that of Long Crichel ... where he built a new parsonage in 1786.

The old parsonage is clearly shown on Isaac Taylor's map, which also reveals that the old village lay along a road, part of which still exists. Sturt must have acted quickly for although he inherited in 1765 the whole village is thought to have disappeared by 1770. The fate of the villagers remains obscure, but it is generally thought that they were rehoused in New Town, that part of Witchampton nearest Crichel. (See map 4)

ENCOMBE

This beautifully situated and secluded country house lies some three miles south-south-west of Corfe Castle at the head of a seaward facing valley. Once a manor and hamlet belonging to Shaftesbury Abbey, it was acquired by the Culliford family shortly after the Dissolution of the Monasteries. Their old manor house was demolished in 1734 after the property had been sold to George Pitt, and his son, John, later built on or near the original site a house once described as 'one of the most elegant houses in these parts'. Traces of the ruins of buildings, including what may have been a chapel, have recently been found in the immediate vicinity of Encombe Farm (now called Encombe Dairy on 1 OS).[3]

KINGSTON LACY

The name is now associated with the house built by Sir Ralph Bankes two miles west of Wimborne in 1663, but there is much evidence to suggest it succeeded an earlier settlement. Like other places in Dorset it is reputed to have been the seat of Saxon Kings, for King Ethelred, Alfred's elder brother, is buried in Wimborne Minster. Domesday Book records it as one of many manors associated with the Minster. Henry I bestowed the large manor of Kingston on a noble and it later passed to John Lacy, Earl of Lincoln, from whom its second name derives. It later passed to John Beaufort, Duke of Somerset, by virtue of his descent from John of Gaunt, and it is thought that the Duke died here in 1444 – he too is buried in the Minster. He left only one daughter, Lady Margaret Beaufort, who later married Edmund Tudor, Earl of Richmond, and became Henry VII's mother.[4] In 1637 the manor, together with Corfe Castle, was purchased by Sir John Bankes. *RCHM* suggests that Kingston was one of four original settlements in the immediate neighbourhood; the others being Bradford (now a farm), Barnsley (also a farm), and Barford (see p. 40), but Kingston's exact site remains uncertain. The settlement including the seat and establishment of the Duke of Somerset must have been considerable, and the fate of the contemporary manor house is told by Hutchins, quoting Leland, who wrote: 'Ther hath bene sins a fair maner place called Kingston-Haul and this is now in a manner clearly defacit. It berith in wrytinges the name of Kingston Lacy.' This was probably also the location of the Chapel of St James which Hutchins records as being neglected in 1504 with only one wall standing. As Lady Margaret Beaufort and her mother left Kingston Lacy after the death of the Duke in 1458 it seems probable that the ancient manor house was allowed to decay and

that the rest of the population then dispersed. It also seems likely that Lady Margaret did not erect the tomb to her parents in Wimborne Minster until after the Chapel of St James had been abandoned. Unfortunately, early maps do not help attempts to locate the precise site of the original settlement, but it may have been near the site of the existing mansion.[5] Against this view is the fact that most early settlements in the area were nearer Wimborne, partly perhaps because most of the open country in the Badbury area was a warren in medieval times and was not enclosed until the late-eighteenth century.[6]

BINGHAM'S MELCOMBE

This was the more easterly of two early settlements in the parish of Melcombe Horsey about ten miles north-east of Dorchester, and it consists today of the parish church, a few farm buildings, and one of the most beautiful manor houses in Dorset; parts of which date back to the time of the village. The site of the old village was immediately to the south of the house and church, and though the reasons for its abandonment are not known, it is thought to have become deserted in about 1400. Though a Royal manor at the time of the Domesday Survey it owes its name to the Bingham family, owners of the manor for more than six hundred years. (See map 8)

MELCOMBE HORSEY

This is the older name for the western settlement in the parish of Melcombe Horsey and its history dates back to Saxon times. Its name derives from the Horsey family who acquired the property by marriage during the reign of Henry VII, but who held it for less than a hundred years. It is now, and more properly, called Higher Melcombe and consists only of the manor house and some adjacent farm buildings. The house is thought to incorporate part of the ancient manor house of Lord Rivers and attached to it is a chapel, said to have been built in the seventeenth century from the ruins of an older parochial chapel.[7] Traces of the old village can still be detected north-west of the house and there is a plan of it in *RCHM* III. (See map 8)

FRIARMAYNE

The house lies on the junction of the Chalk and the Reading Beds in the parish of West Knighton. Hutchins records that 'here was a preceptory belonging to the Knights Hospitallers. Here they had an ancient manor house. It was one of the commandries of the order. When it was first erected is uncertain but seems to have been before 1305.' It is not, however, mentioned in any list of preceptories in 1434. The settlement attached to it, or which perhaps succeeded it, lay just west of the present house and there is a plan of it in *RCHM* II. (See map 9)

FROME BELET

This is the name of a now obsolete parish half-a-mile north of West Stafford, whose name derives from a William Belet who held the manor at the time of Domesday Book. There is now no trace of the old village, but it seems possible that Stafford House may stand on the site.

FROME WHITFIELD

Immediately north of Dorchester this was once a parish with its own rectory dating back to 1327, but in 1610 its revenues were annexed to Holy Trinity, Dorchester, because the settlement had by then become depopulated. Since 1894 it has been part of the parish of Stinsford. The estate was once owned by Denzil Holles, son of the Earl of Clare and Dorchester's Member of Parliament in the mid-seventeenth century. It seems probable that the old village had disappeared and the manor house declined into a farmhouse long before Holles acquired it. In 1799 the property was purchased by William Lewis Henning and a new house built on the site of the manor. Stones from old buildings, some clearly from a church, make it clear that the old village lay within the extensive gardens laid out by Henning; probably immediately to the south of Frome House.

HANFORD

There is still a small parish of this name lying between the River Stour and the road between Child Okeford and Iwerne Stepleton, but the old village, which according to Hutchins lay north of the house, had in his time been 'de-populated beyond memory'. Settlement remains have been recorded which place it just south of the church, in which case it is partly covered by Hanford House, now a school. (See map 10)

IWERNE STEPLETON

Though still a parish, and once a village, nothing remains of the latter except part of the eleventh-century church. On 1 OS it is marked by the name Stepleton House in antique lettering, and the house is reputed to stand on the site of the old village – deserted by 1662. There are some signs of ground disturbance east of the house which possibly indicate the site of other old buildings. In 1745 the estate was bought by Julines Beckford 'of Jamaica', who at once began to rebuild the existing house. His son Peter, author of the classic *Thoughts on Hunting* and one of the founders of modern fox-hunting, continued the rebuilding, adding the handsome brick stables for his horses and hounds. (See map 10)

KINGSTON MAURWARD

The key to this old village, which lay in Stinsford parish about two miles east of Dorchester, is that the name now applies to two country houses. The older of these, the Old Manor House, dates from the sixteenth century, and, though for some time converted into tenements, it has recently been beautifully restored. It may be supposed that the old village stood close to this house. The other house, Kingston House, now much better known, was built in about 1720 on higher ground a little to the west of the Old Manor House by one of the Pitts, after his marriage to Lora Grey, heiress to the estate. Extensive and lavish gardens were eventually laid out round the new house, but there is no evidence to suggest that they impinged on the old village. The old road from West Stafford running northward toward the upper Piddle valley once ran through the old settlement, but when the new house was built it was realigned to the east.

LEWESTON

This is a small parish between Lillington and Longburton consisting of Leweston Park, which

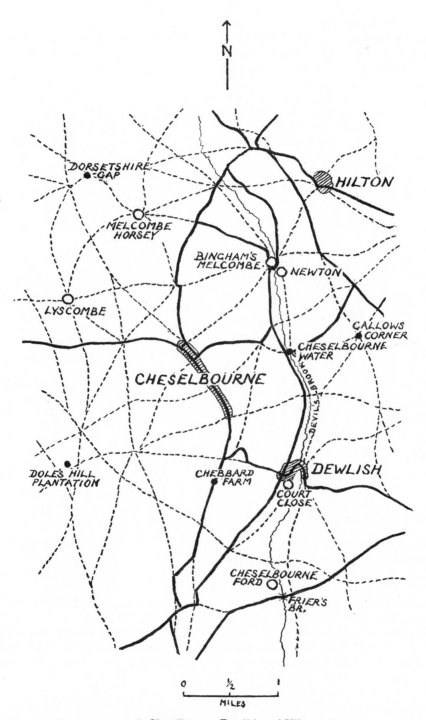

N

DORSETSHIRE GAP

HILTON

MELCOMBE HORSEY

BINGHAM'S MELCOMBE

NEWTON

LYSCOMBE

GALLOWS CORNER

CHESELBOURNE WATER

CHESELBOURNE

DEVIL'S BROOK

DOLE'S HILL PLANTATION

CHEBBARD FARM

DEWLISH

COURT CLOSE

CHESELBOURNE FORD

FRIER'S BR.

0   ½   1
MILES

MAP 8. Cheselbourne, Dewlish and Hilton

was enlarged in the nineteenth century. Previously the ancient manor house of the Fitzjames family had been demolished to be replaced by a house standing in Hutchins time; this is now a school. The church stands to the north-east of the house and the old village presumably lay nearby. Hutchins seems to indicate that there were 33 manorial tenants in his time and quotes Leland as writing that the Leweston family had owned it since before the Norman Conquest. The name is shown in antique lettering on 6 OS but there are now no traces of the old village. (See map 11)

RANSTON

Ranston House, thought to have been built by Sir Thomas Freke in the early seventeenth century, stands on the outskirts of Iwerne Courtney, or Shroton as it is now more commonly called. The old village, shown on Taylor's map by his conventional signs for old foundations and on 6 OS 1902 by the site of a chapel, lay to the south of the house. It seems probable that the village was either deserted before Freke bought the property or when he began the construction of the house. The house was partially rebuilt in 1750, and in 1781 was bought by Peter William Baker, the Portmans' agent at Bryanston, and after whom Baker Street in London is named. (See map 10)

SMEDMORE

This country house, which stands a little to the east of Kimmeridge, illustrates many aspects of Dorset local history. It was once one of three parish settlements, Great Kimmeridge, Smedmore and Little Kimmeridge or Chaldecote (q.v.): of these the first survives as the existing village, the second is a country house, and the third has vanished. Smedmore's history goes back to Saxon times, and it has been identified as the 'Metmore' of Domesday Book. This later became modified to 'Smedmore' and gave its name to the family which held it between the reigns of Edward I and Richard II. In about 1450 it passed to the Clavells, and a member of the family, said to have been in Dorset since shortly after the Norman Conquest, still lives there. The remains of the old

village were probably obliterated in about 1700 when the house was rebuilt and the grounds redesigned and enlarged.[8] (See map 15)

STINSFORD

The parish of this name lies just north-east of Dorchester, between Charminster and Puddletown. Its history pre-dates the Norman Conquest but just how large a village it was before 'the manor became extinct, the vill depopulated, and only the church, manor house and parsonage remains' is hard to tell. Today the settlement mainly comprises a large, comparatively modern, farmstead. The manor house has suffered considerable change, but parts apparently belong to a building described in Coker's time as 'much decayed'. The house was rebuilt in about 1700 when it became the property of the Strangways family, to whom it still belongs, and it seems likely that the old village disappeared when the park was laid out. The old settlement lay along the old road on the north bank of the River Frome.

STOCK GAYLARD

This Saxon village, between Bishop's Caundle and Lydlinch, was formerly a parish, but of the village now only the church remains. It is the centre of a large estate with a deer park, and the old village, of which no traces remain, may be covered by Stock House. The house dates from the early eighteenth century, but whilst Taylor's map shows the house as south of the church, the present building stands to its north. The old village had its own open fields and is thought to have been depopulated in the fifteenth century. (See map 6)

THORNHILL

Though held by one of the King's thanes at the time of Domesday Book, little is known about the old village except that it was once part of a tithing and manor in the large parish of Stalbridge. In Richard II's reign it was held by John Thornhull de Hargrove. Leland makes more than one reference to it, notably: 'from Stapleford onto Thornhill, a myle by good ground enclosed. Here dwellith Master Thornhill an ancient gentleman'. Towards the end of the seventeenth century the Thornhills sold the estate, but it was rebought by another member of the family, the artist Sir James Thornhill, who then built a new house on the property. The old village, which probably fell into decay when the Thornhills moved to Woolland, acquired from Henry VIII in 1540, lay on the old road from Hazelbury Bryan to Stalbridge by Lydlinch. The local road pattern was much altered by the enclosure of Stalbridge Common and by the construction of the turnpike to the west of Thornhill. (See map 6)

WATERSTON

The site of a deserted village has been found on the south side of the county road, just to the west of Waterston House. The house was built in about 1660 and its relationship with the village has yet to be established.

WEST WOODYATES

Though once a separate parish, this now lies in the parish of Pentridge. It has been suggested that a settlement existed here in Roman times, but by the end of the eighteenth century the village had become reduced to a single farmhouse. The present house is known as West Woodyates Manor.[9] Traces of an old garden layout have recently been reported.

WINTERBORNE CAME

So named because of its association with the Abbey of St Etienne at Caen in Normandy, Winterborne Came is now remembered because for many years it was the home of the Dorset poet William Barnes, whose picturesque thatched rectory stands on the Dorchester/Broadmayne road. But by Barnes's time the old village (which may have included a nunnery) had long since disappeared. Hutchins, writing in 1750, shortly after the construction of Came House, described the village as 'now almost depopulated, consisting only of three or four houses'. The few houses must have soon been demolished, for Taylor's map of 1765 shows the church and mansion on the west side of the old road from Dorchester to Culliford Tree and only a solitary farmhouse on the east side. This too no longer exists. Today there is a little estate settlement between Came House and the church, but it seems unlikely that this has any connexion with the ancient village; the site of which remains in some doubt. There are extensive settlement remains (well described in *RCHM* II) between Chapel Hill Coppice and Home Wood, but whether these represent the old village or whether still other remains are concealed by Came House, is not known. The fact that a number of old roads once met a little to the east of the present buildings may be relevant to the position of the old village, though this too is uncertain. (See map 5)

5

Villages now Represented by Farmsteads

The old settlements which survive by name, and of which the sites are known, but which are now represented by one, or rarely more, farmsteads and farms, are many, and it is not easy to decide which of them merit mention in this chapter. Information about the early history of most of them is scanty. Some are known to have existed in Saxon times, while others are first recorded in documents of the twelfth and thirteenth centuries. Judging from estimates of population it is probably fair to regard these as having been, at some time and in relation to the contemporary population distribution, small settlements. Of the remainder most seem to have arisen as small peripheral or satellite settlements through the process of assarting (see p. 4) either while the open fields were still in existence, or more particularly perhaps, following their enclosure in the sixteenth and seventeenth centuries.

The Poole Basin

The Poole Basin North (PBN)

WILKSWORTH

This is now in the parish of Colehill, north of Wimborne and east of the River Allen, and has been identified as once part of a Saxon Hundred. Hutchins refers to it when quoting the bounds of 'Wimborne Chase' in the reign of Edward I. The farm buildings date from about 1500 but have been much altered.

The Poole Basin Central (PBC)

BHOMPSTON

This is a large farmstead about half-a-mile east of Lower Bockhampton and has been known by several other names, amongst them Frome Bonvyle. Once a manor and hamlet, it owed its importance to its position on the River Frome (which can here be easily crossed) and to the old road on the river's north bank which ran through Kingston Maurward.

GALTON

Once a hamlet and tithing, Galton is now a farmstead half-a-mile east of Owermoigne on the old West Chaldon to Moreton road. Settlement remains are recorded close to the present buildings and Isaac Taylor's map show houses stretching for some half-a-mile along the old road. (See map 9)

HETHFELTON

This is described by Hutchins as once a manor, farm and grange belonging to Bindon Abbey two miles north-west of East Stoke. This would place it on the east bank of a tiny stream called the Holy Stream which runs south into the River Frome – in the exact spot where its name now appears on 1 OS. The name first appears in Domesday Book; and as Hethfelton Farm,

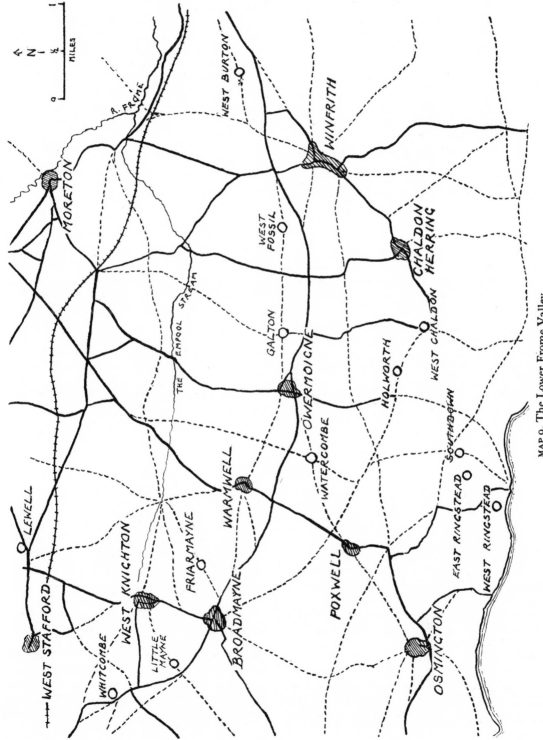

MAP 9. The Lower Frome Valley

which lies 400 yards north of Bindon Abbey on the north side of the Frome, has traces of six-teenth-century building, it would seem to be the most likely site of the original settlement.

LEWELL

Sometimes called East Stafford, Lewell is now represented by a splendid old farmstead called Lower Lewell Farm and by Lewell Mill on the line of an ancient and important crossing of the Frome valley. It was surveyed in Domesday Book as two parcels and in later times is thought to have belonged to the Knights Tem-plars. (See map 9)

LITTLE MAYNE

Once part of the land given by King Athelstan to his religious foundation at Milton Abbas, Little Mayne lies just off the road between Dorchester and Broadmayne (A352) in the parish of West Knighton. The old village is now represented by a farmstead which stands on or close to its original site.[1] Maps suggest that a small field north of the main road called Cemetery Field, and said never to have been ploughed, was the old burial ground.[2] (See map 9)

RUSHTON

A royal manor in Domesday Book, Rushton is an excellent example of the effect road changes have had on old villages. Until the formation of the Wareham Turnpike Trust it lay on the main Wareham/Wool road, but when the turnpike was built it bypassed the village, with the result that it gradually lost its importance. It now con-sists of a large farmstead.

The Poole Basin South (PBS)

OWER

Ower lies on the shores of Poole Harbour north of Rempstone, and was once the 'chief if not the only quay for the exporting of stone' until it was superseded by Swanage in the early eigh-teenth century. It thus must have had a long, close and important association with the Pur-beck stone industry. It marks the terminal for several old roads from the quarries of east Pur-beck, amongst them the Marbler's Road from Corfe Castle, along which much of the Purbeck marble was carried. At its height Ower must have been busy and prosperous, but apart from traces of a causeway or mole into the harbour, only a few scattered buildings still remain.

The Chalk

The Northern Chalk (NCH)

ALLHALLOWS WIMBORNE

Sometimes known as Wimborne All Saints, All-hallows Wimborne is now represented by All-hallows Farm and its surrounding buildings. It was formerly a parish and the site of the church is known. Hutchins rather confusingly notes that 'in 1291 the church of Wimborne Karentham seems to have been the mother church and that of Wimborne St Giles is stiled only the Chapel of St Giles.' He was perhaps referring to the old church, united with that of Wimborne St Giles in 1733 and then pulled down. Running due

west from the present farmstead is a rough road called the 'Coach Road' on 6 OS 1902. This was once part of the old highway between Salis-bury and Dorchester by way of Cranborne. (See map 4)

BERE PEVEREL

The name is now attached to a large farm-stead, better known as Barford, about a mile south-west of Kingston Lacy. The old settle-ment is shown by Isaac Taylor and described by Hutchins as consisting of two farms on the north bank of the River Stour east of Sturmin-ster Marshall. It is also shown on Speed's early seventeenth-century maps. The settlement stood on the river bank at the top of a sharp loop at a point where the river can, or at least could, be forded when its level was low. The spot is now occupied by a ruined seventeenth-century farmhouse.

GUSSAGE ST ANDREW

Here, according to Hutchins, was 'anciently a distinct chapel of ease to the mother church at Iwerne Minster but in later times it seems to have been included in the chapelry of Hanley'. It is now a large farmstead in the parish of Sixpenny Handley and the chapel, which has some interesting wall paintings, is still used. (See map 4)

MONKTON UP WIMBORNE

This scattered hamlet lies on the north bank of the River Allen, which rises just beyond it. Although it has a small modern church and the remains of an ancient chapel it seems unlikely that it was ever a parish. Spelt Opewinburne, it is mentioned in Domesday Book. It has been suggested that its first name derives from its later association with Cranborne Priory. (See map 4)

NUTFORD LOCKEY

This appears to be now represented by France Farm, a large farmstead just inside the parish of Stourpaine on the south side of the A350 between Blandford and Durweston, which was once known as either Nutford Lockey or Nutford Barnard. Its position suggests it once was larger, for it stands on the old road from Bulbarrow to Ashmore and near a ford on the River Stour. (See map 10)

PRESTON

This has been identified as an old manor.[3] Lying a little south of Iwerne Minster it is now represented by Preston House. *RCHM* IV suggests that it was one of the two original settlements in the parish of Iwerne Minster.

TARRANT LAUNCESTON

This is one of the more familiar shrunken villages, and the old settlement is now represented by a dairy farm and some nearby remains, amongst them those of a chapel, though the parish as a whole is probably as populous as at any time in its history. It was once part of the endowment of the Benedictine Nunnery of the Holy Trinity at Caen founded by Maud, William the Conqueror's sister.

TARRANT PRESTON

In the late eighteenth-century this was still a hamlet in Tarrant Crawford (*q.v.*). It seems probable that the original settlement stood near the present Preston Farm, past which an important old road between Christchurch and Shaftesbury (known locally as Wimborne Way) once ran. Though no settlement remains have been recorded, *RCHM* IV regards it as one of the two medieval settlements of Tarrant Rushton.

WOODCUTTS

Standing midway between Sixpenny Handley and Tollard Royal, Woodcutts is another example of the results of turnpike construction. Once a small settlement centred round Manor Farm and dating back to 1244, it became bypassed when the Cranborne and New Forest Turnpike Trust was formed to build a new road to the north of the old. There are some interesting suggestions of old remains, especially near Manor Farm, and the name Woodcutts is also given to the Romano-British village on Woodcutts Common.

The Central Chalk (CCH)

BAGBER

This is now a large farmstead on the Milborne Brook a mile north of Milborne St Andrew. Even its present appearance suggests it was once larger and settlement remains have been reported north of the existing buildings. The old road on the east bank of the Brook ran through it, as also did a more important highway that crossed Dorset by way of Cranborne and Cerne Abbas. (See map 3)

BARCOMBE

Now represented by a farmstead, this was once a small village standing on the east side of the River Piddle slightly north of Alton Pancras.

Settlement remains have been found half-a-mile north of Alton Pancras church, and it seems probable that there was once a true gap between the two places.

BURTON

This is now the name of an old settlement standing at the northern end of the Frome valley crossing due north of Dorchester. An inn and farmstead still survive, and until recently there was a working mill. The buildings stand on the Old Sherborne Road (itself based on a pre-Roman ridgeway) and the village was probably at its largest soon after the old road became a turnpike in about 1760.

KNIGHTON

This is the name of an old parish and church which adjoined Durweston. The two churches were united in 1381, perhaps because Knighton was already in decay, and its church is now parish church of Durweston. A group of buildings still bear the name, but as these are not connected with the old village they may not indicate its site. (See map 10)

LITTLETON

Standing about a mile south of Blandford and mentioned in Domesday Book, this was once a separate parish adjoining that of Blandford St Mary. Settlement remains have been recorded immediately east of Littleton House, but the name is now that of a group of buildings along the A350.

LYSCOMBE

The old settlement lies on the old road, parts of which are still very clear, between Milton Abbas and Cerne Abbas, about midway between the two, and it seems probable that it was closely associated with the wayfaring life of earlier medieval times. It is now represented by a large farmstead which includes a chapel and a priest's house. The village was given by King Athelstan to his new foundation at Milton Abbas and it remained in the hands of the church until the Dissolution of the Monasteries.

MILBORNE DEVEREL

See p. 12 above.

MUSTON

An old manor house and extensive farm buildings now represent this deserted village in the upper Piddle valley. Once a manor and hamlet given by King Edgar to Cerne Abbey, it came into the possession of the Churchill family during the reign of James I.

QUARLESTON

Sometimes known as Winterborne Quarlston, this old village in the North Winterborne valley is still represented by a group of farm buildings. It is thought to take its name from the Quarrel family, who were amongst its early holders. There are settlement remains just south-west of the old farmhouse. An old road between Milton Abbey and Blandford once crossed the valley here, and parts of it can still be seen south of the farm.

THORNICOMBE

Hutchins describes Thornicombe as 'anciently a hamlet ... the vill is entirely depopulated and only a barn remaining'. It was once a detached part of Turnworth parish and the site is now represented by a farm in Thornicombe Bottom, a mile east of Winterborne Clenston. The old settlement was on a road from Milton Abbas to Tarrant Monkton, part of which still survives as a length of county road past Sparrowbush Farm. (See map 10)

WINTERBORNE TOMSON

The settlement has long been familiar as a shrunken village thanks to its charming church, which stands in its own graveyard and is still occasionally used for worship. It now consists of a large farmstead and seventeenth-century house, but modern buildings rather spoil its appearance and character.

WOLFETON

This is well known for the splendid manor house built by the Trenchards in about 1500 on the edge of the Frome meadows about half-a-

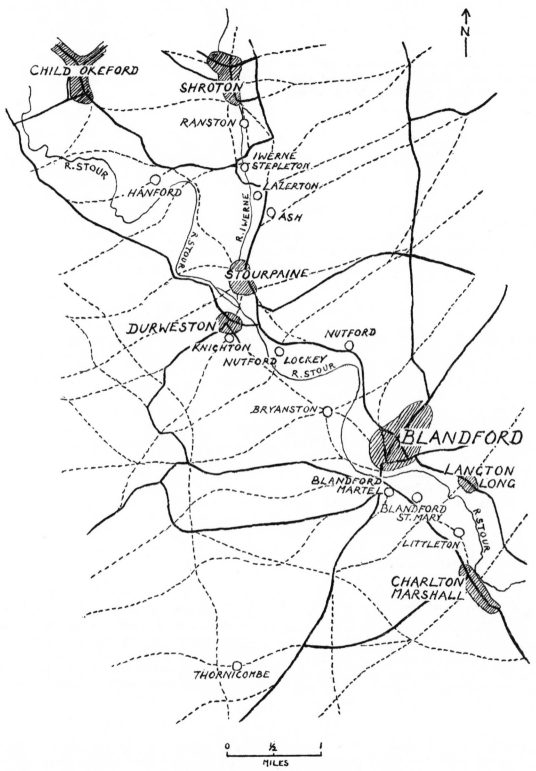

MAP 10. Blandford and the Iwerne Valley

mile south of Charminster. Hutchins mentions that the old vill has long been 'extinguished and depopulated'. Settlement remains have been recorded to the north of the house.

The Southern Chalk (SCH)

FROME WHITWELL

This was once a hamlet but is now little more than a farmstead, lying close to the River Frome at the foot of Fordington Bottom about a mile north-west of Dorchester. It is perhaps just as well that 1 OS no longer names the place, because earlier maps call it Whitfield Farm – a misnomer which it seems to have acquired, perhaps in confusion with Frome Whitfield across the river, when the 1811 OS was published. Its correct name of Frome Whitwell derives from the remarkable springs of pure chalk water that emerge from the foot of the steep western scarp of Poundbury Hill. There is good reason to sup-

pose that there has been a settlement of some kind here ever since the days of Maiden Castle.

WATERCOMBE

Hutchins describes Watercombe as a farm, but this is an inadequate description for one of the most interesting of old villages now reduced to farmsteads. It lies on the south side of the A352 south of Warmwell, and is today almost the only inhabited place in the small parish that still bears its name. It was once a manor and before the Norman Conquest was held by a Saxon called Aluric. Today Watercombe is a splendid example of an old-time farmstead; with a large thatched farmhouse, satellite cottages, and extensive farm buildings – amongst them a charming old granary, traditionally the site of a chapel. There is good evidence that other buildings once existed. It stood at the crossing of two roads; one that ran inland from Ringstead Bay (probably a popular smuggling route), and the other from Owermoigne to Poxwell and Weymouth. (See map 9 and plate 2)

The Northern Vales

The Blackmoor Vale North (BVN)

BEDCHESTER

Formerly a Saxon hamlet belonging to Milton Abbey, Bedchester stands midway between East Orchard and Fontmell Magna. Modern buildings now blur the outline of the old settlement, but it was almost certainly centred on the crossing of the Fontmell Magna/Wincanton road and the road (in part an ancient ridgeway) between Shaftesbury and Childe Okeford. 400 yards west of the crossing there is another small cluster of buildings centred on St Andrew's Farm. These once stood on the through road leading to the chapel at Hartgrove (see p. 63) and may have been a separate village or a detached part of Bedchester itself. (See map 17)

BUGLEY

Standing two miles south-west of Gillingham and described by Coker as one of two 'little

obscure parishes', Bugley is said to have once had a chapel. At the beginning of this century it consisted of a scattered group of buildings set amongst orchards, but no settlement remains have been noted.

HAM

Hutchins refers to this as the second of the 'obscure parishes' mentioned by Coker, and the details indicate that it lay south of Gillingham and south of the River Stour. The name Ham Common is now connected to a built-up area south-east of Gillingham on the B3081, and this may indicate the whereabouts of the old settlement.

LANGHAM

This consists of an extensive group of farms and other buildings which lie about two miles due west of Gillingham. Settlement remains covering some ten acres have been found to the north of Higher Langham Farm.

LITTLE KINGTON

Little Kington lies north-west of the village of West Stour in the parish of that name and is generally regarded as an ancient settlement, albeit a small one, which is represented by the farm bearing its name.[4]

PRESTON

This, the most northerly of several Prestons in Dorset, consists of an old manor, hamlet and farm now represented by Pierston Farm. It lies on the old Gillingham/Silton road and twelfth and thirteenth-century pottery has been found on the site of the old settlement.

THORTON

Once the capital settlement of its own parish, Thorton (or Thornton) lies about two miles north of Hinton St Mary. It seems probable that the chapel of St Martin was desecrated and converted into a farm building during the Reformation, when the parish was absorbed into that of Marnhull. The site of the old village, now a farmstead, is a slightly raised rectangular platform partially surrounded by the remains of a moat. The village is thought to have been abandoned in the fifteenth century and there are settlement remains in the immediate vicinity of the present farmhouse. (See map 17 and plate 3)

The Blackmoor Vale West (BVW)

BERE MARSH

North of Hayward Bridge near Shillingstone and west of the River Stour, the old settlement stood on the old Shillingstone/Hammoon road. It once consisted of a manor, hamlet and mill. 6 OS 1902 shows a square moat and other earthworks on the west side of the railway, and in 1847 some remains of what were thought to be the 'Old Manor' were found.

CHITCOMBE

This small hamlet lies half-a-mile due east of Woolland church. The first recording of the name dates from 1327 and there are settlement remains just west of the present farm. 'An Ana-baptist meeting house was built here about 1723', perhaps because of the seclusion afforded by the site.

FONT LE ROI

This interesting old settlement, sometimes known as Fauntleroy's Marsh, lies about half-a-mile north west of Caundle Marsh in the parish of Folke, and today consists of an irregular group of buildings centred round a farmyard. The north wing includes the remnants of a fifteenth-century gatehouse, and the charming house on the south-western corner (which dates from about 1600) contains one room with an original plaster ceiling. Font le Roi was once a manor belonging to the Bishops of Sarum, but from the middle of the fourteenth to the end of the seventeenth centuries it was held by the Fauntleroys, a family described by Coker as 'men of no mean antiquity'. Hutchins also mentions it, calling it 'a pretty large, low, and very grotesque building, entirely of stone, and perhaps one of the most ancient houses in the county'. (See map 11)

HARTLEY

Now consisting of little more than Hartley Farm, Hartley lies just inside the parish of Minterne Magna. The farm stands close to the scene of the great sixteenth-century landslip from High Stoy, an event which may have hastened the decline of the settlement. Hartley had close links with the De La Lynde family, best known for its connexion with the thirteenth-century story of Whitehart Silver, which Hutchins relates in his account of the Vale or Forest of Blackmoor or White Hart.[5]

LYDLINCH BARET (HYDES)

Once a manor dating back to the reign of Richard II, the buildings of the medieval settlement stand on the old road from Okeford Fitzpaine to Stourton Caundle. The name is little used today, and the place is now more commonly known as Hydes.

NEWLAND

Now in the parish of Glanvilles Wootton, Newland was once a manor to which Hutchins gives the alternative names of Newton-Montacute

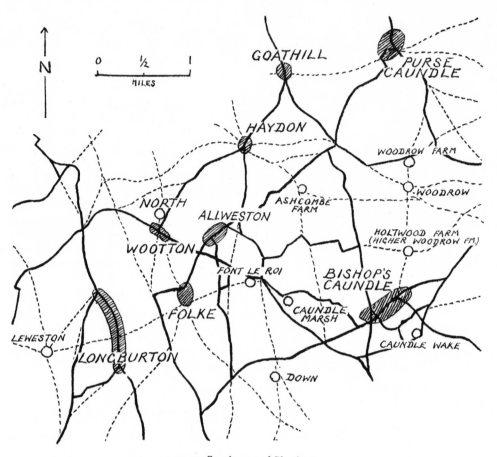

MAP 11. South-east of Sherborne

and Blackmoor-Manor; the latter is of interest because it may explain the otherwise puzzling name of Blackmoor Ford Bridge over the Caundle Brook. In the opinion of *RCHM* the old Newland Manor centred on the ancient Round Chimneys Farm, long associated with the Churchill family, but the name has now become transferred, apparently deliberately, to an area about a mile to the south-east which was enclosed and laid out along what is now called Newland Lane, probably in the first half of the nineteenth century.

PLUMBER

Lying on the River Divelish about a mile south of Fifehead St Quintin, Plumber comprises a fine old manor house and extensive farm build-

ings. It is in a prominent tongue of the present parish of Lydlinch and may once have been a separate entity. Hutchins gives an engraving of the place which is a delightful picture of the rural scene of his time. Between the two places mentioned there is the site of a Roman villa. Two important old roads, from Bulbarrow to Stalbridge and from Okeford Fitzpaine to Bishop's Caundle, ran through Plumber. (See map 6)

THURNET

This was a small hamlet, sometimes called Thurnhead, in the parish of Mappowder. It seems reasonable to suppose that the latter name became phonetically changed to the former, and that this in turn gave its name to Thurnwood Farm and Dairy which are in the

1. MILBORNE ST. ANDREW (see pp. 12-16)
  Aerial view from the south, 1974. Cole's Farm is in the topmost group of buildings, with Cole's Lane running left from it. The old road between Winterborne Whitechurch and Dewlish, now mostly part of the old turnpike A 354, runs across the upper half of the picture, and the older road to Dorchester from the east is parallel to it south of the church (centre left). Running down from the top right hand corner is the road from Milton Abbas, which now ends as the approach to the house of Manor Farm. Note the old gate pillars where the two latter roads cross. The conspicuous chalk road running south between the house of Manor Farm and its farm buildings is an accommodation road to Snag Lane replacing the continuation of the road from Milton Abbas down the valley to Ashley Barn and beyond.

2.*(Top left)* WATERCOMBE (see p. 44)

Aerial view from the south, 1974. The two continuous south-north hedgelines right and left of the buildings mark the boundaries of the civil parish, almost the whole of which is covered by the picture. The road between Dorchester and Wareham, A 352, crosses the centre of the photograph.

3.*(Above)* MARSHWOOD CASTLE (see p. 50)

Aerial view from the north, 1974. The old site, now occupied by Lodge House Farm, is in the centre of the upper half of the picture at the end of the blind road leading to it from the cross roads at Taphouse Farm. The ancient motte is between the two right hand farm buildings. The road between Valehouse Farm and Sansom's Cross runs through the cross roads, and the branch running right from it passes by Frog House Farm. The sinuous lines of bushes in the upper half of the picture mark part of the R.Char and its tributaries.

4.*(Left)* WYTHERSTON (see p. 50)

Aerial view from the north-west, 1974. The farmstead representing the old village is at the end of the white road leading off the road between Powerstock and Mount Pleasant, part of which is seen at the bottom of the picture. The buildings in the left bottom corner are modern. Running to the right from the corner of the larger wood in the upper half of the picture is the line of the railway between Maiden Newton and Bridport.

5. WINTERBORNE WHITECHURCH (see p. 62)

Aerial view from the north-west, 1974. The farms in the upper half of the picture make up Lower Street through which the pre-turnpike road between Blandford and Dorchester ran. The turnpike, now A 354, runs across the picture from the middle point of the right hand margin, and joining it in the village is the road from Milton Abbas on which the church stands. The conspicuous white road lower left is the approach to La Lee Farm and left of it is new housing. The course of the North Winterborne is marked by the left hand long row of trees and bushes in the centre; the deserted medieval village straddled the part of it nearer Lower Street. The right hand line of trees marks the present road which replaced that which ran through the old village.

6. WHITCOMBE (see p. 63)

Aerial view from the south, 1974. The church stands a little apart on the north and the building nearest the road on the south is the farm house. The pre-turnpike road from Dorchester to Broadmayne is outside the picture on the left. The first line of the turnpike is marked by the line of trees north of the church and continues south as the road A 352. The conspicuous dog-leg in the present road is a later turnpike development.

7.*(Above)* TODBER (see p. 65)

Aerial view from the south, 1974. The parish church is prominent standing alone on the short length of road which now joins Church Lane (running across the bottom of the picture) and Shave Lane (running across the middle). South-east of the church, Church Lane is now only a public footpath where its line crosses the site of an old quarry, now occupied by a County Council Road Depot and its buildings. In the left-hand bottom corner of the picture this old road now affords access to a series of bungalows. At the right-hand end of Shave Lane and on its north side is the 18th century Manor Farm; and at the left-hand end, also on the north side, is a row of cottages built in 1868, when the population of the parish was at its highest, and now prolonged eastward by three bungalows. On the south side of the road are two of the cottages built along the new road at the time of enclosure. Between these and Manor Farm, again on the north side of the road, is a house, probably about a hundred years old, which is now the Post Office.

8.*(Left)* ADBER (see p. 67)

Aerial view looking north, 1974. Part of the Castle Cary-Yeovil railway is seen in the top left hand corner, and the inner of the two parallel hedgelines in the top right hand corner marks the old turnpike, now B 3148, between Sherborne and Marston Magna. The road running north to the upper right hand edge of the picture is part of that between Trent and Rimpton. All the buildings along this are modern and the old village clusters round the branches of the side road off it.

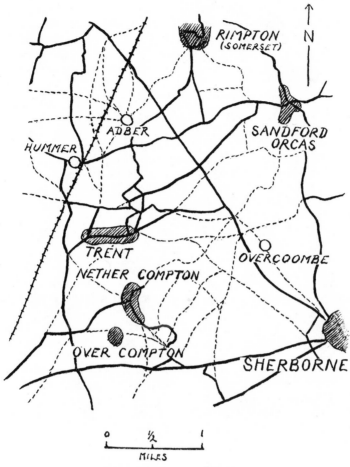

MAP 12. North-west of Sherborne

south-west of the parish. This was part of the great area to the west of the Armswell/Mappowder road which Isaac Taylor calls Thurnwood Common and shows as uninhabited. Since its enclosure Thurnwood Farm and its associates have stood on it, but they are not likely to represent any old settlement. The original settlement may have been at or west of Armswell, which dates back to the fourteenth century and the immediate neighbourhood of the little wood called Aldermore might well repay careful attention.

WOODROW

Woodrow dates from the fourteenth century and lies in the parish of Stourton Caundle. Evidence suggests that there was once a through road between Purse Caundle and Bishop's Caundle along the east side of Plumley Wood, and along this route are three sites incorporating the name Woodrow: Woodrow Farm, Lower Woodrow, and Higher Woodrow Farm (recently renamed Holtwood Farm). Of these Lower Woodrow, which stands on a little brook running east into Stourton Caundle, is a decayed group of buildings which give the impression of having once been larger. It is perhaps significant that the old road stopped at Lower Woodrow and that there are three old stone bridges in the immediate vicinity, indicating that communications in the area were once better. It is also worth noting that the land south of Holtwood Farm seems to have been enclosed in an unusually artificial way; this may have marked the final decline of the old settlement, cutting it off from Bishop's Caundle to the south. (See map 11)

WOOLCOMBE MATRAVERS

Described by Hutchins as a tithing, manor and hamlet belonging to Melbury Bubb, and once with a chapel, this is a puzzling place because although the name Woolcombe appears several times on 6 OS 1903 there is no indication of where the old village may have been. Hutchins includes an engraving of a country house, new in his time, and of surpassing ugliness, and the site of this, and of a successor, is now Woolcombe Farm. Some indications suggest that the old village may have been where Redford Farm now stands on one of the headwaters of the River Wriggle, though this is now just in Batcombe parish. Another possibility is that it stood near Higher Woolcombe Dairy, parts of which date back to the seventeenth century. (See map 7)

Trans-Yeo (TY)

HUMMER

This is an odd little extension of the parish of Trent. The first known reference to it dates back to 1091. Like neighbouring Adber (see p. 67) and the rest of the parish of Trent it did not become part of Dorset until 1896. (See map 12)

OVERCOOMBE

Overcoombe today consists of Coombe Farm, a farmstead lying about a mile north-west of Sherborne on the east side of the Sherborne/Marston Magna road. According to Hutchins it once had a chapel, and is referred to as one of the six tithings of the parish of Sherborne.[6] (See map 12)

WYKE

Once belonging to the Abbots of Sherborne, who had a 'retiring place' there, Wyke lies in the parish of Castleton abut three-quarters of a mile east of Bradford Abbas church. Today it consists of a large farmhouse and a remarkable range of tithe-barns, attributed to the sixteenth century. If this date is correct they must have been built shortly before the Dissolution of the Monasteries or when the property first passed into lay ownership. Unfortunately the construction of the railway in the nineteenth century divided the house from the barns. Wyke is now remarkably isolated, but it once lay on two old roads.

The Western Vales

The Axe Vales (AV)

CHILDHAY

Once a tithing of Broadwindsor, Childhay stands in the narrow neck that connects the two parts of the parish. It is now a large and pleasantly situated farmhouse, but its history goes back at least as far as the reign of Edward III. Much of it was burnt during the Civil War, but thankfully the fine fifteenth-century entrance porch still survives.

HOLDITCH

The parish of Thorncombe extends over much of the Axe Vales, yet to most people in Dorset it remains unfamiliar; partly because it is a western extension and partly because it was not absorbed into the county until 1844. It has one large and compact village, Thorncombe, but the rest of the population live in scattered hamlets and farms. The name Holditch attaches to three distinct places: the hamlet of Holditch, Holditch Court, and the rather more distant sixteenth-century Lower Holditch Farm. The hamlet, which once stood on the old road linking Hawkchurch with Forde Abbey, includes Higher Holditch Farm, Manor Farm, and a seventeenth-century inn. Holditch Court also stands on the old road and now consists of a single farmstead and numerous outbuildings.

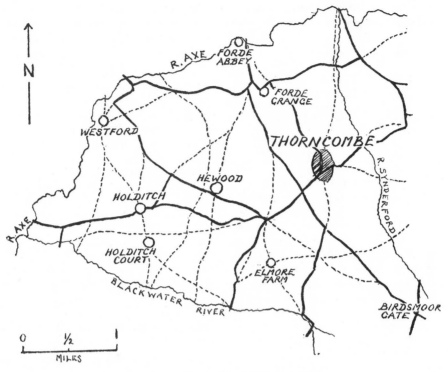

MAP 13. The parish of Thorncombe

They include the gatehouse of a sixteenth-century mansion and the spectacular ruins of a fourteenth-century tower of a fortified manor house belonging to the Brook family. Life-size brasses of Thomas Brook and his wife can still be seen in Thorncombe Church. The family were well-known Dorset landholders and was later ennobled. (See map 13)

WESTFORD

Several buildings bear this name (Westford Farm, Westford Mill and Westford Park) and all of them stand on the old Hawkchurch/Chard road to the south of Chard Junction. Westford's importance lies in its connexion with the history of Forde Abbey. In 1132 Richard de Redvers, lord of Okehampton, persuaded a small group of monks at the Cistercian Abbey of Waverley to move to a new building on land on Dartmoor which he had given them. They found this so bleak and so hard to farm that

after his death they decided to return to Waverley. On the way they passed through Thorncombe, where de Redvers' sister held the manor of West Ford. She offered them land on the manor in exchange for that on Dartmoor. This they accepted, remaining in West Ford until Forde Abbey had been completed. (See map 13)

The Marshwood Vales (MV)

ATRIM

A tiny, scattered hamlet in the parish of Symondsbury, Atrim was once large enough to merit its own entry in Domesday Book. Prior to the Norman Conquest it was held by Abbotsbury Abbey. Maps show a bridge, farm and cottages as bearing the name and this, combined with the probability that Atrim Gore

House was built in the fifteenth century, suggest a long and continuous history.

MARSHWOOD CASTLE

This is the correct name of an ancient site, one-and-a-half miles north of Whitchurch Canonicorum, on which Lodge House Farm now stands. The castle was the seat of the Barony of Mandeville of Marshwood throughout much of the thirteenth century.[7] Surrounded by the remains of its moat, there still survive the site of a chapel of St Mary, a small motte on which are the ruins of a simple stone keep, and traces of other buildings. Hutchins states that its first holder came over with William the Conqueror and the size of the castle precinct suggests that it must have once housed a substantial population. It seems to have fallen into disuse in the late Middle Ages, but its chapel remained a chapel of ease to Whitchurch Canonicorum until it was destroyed during the Civil War. The castle's history would repay further investigation, for it seems remarkable that a castle should have been built so soon after the Norman Conquest in a clay vale which still remains one of the most remote corners of Dorset. (See plate 4)

The Powerstock Vales (PV)

MAPPERCOMBE

Mappercombe was once a manor, with a chapel and hamlet, in the tithing of Nettlecombe in the parish of Powerstock, but by the eighteenth century the fifteenth-century manor house had become a farm. The settlement was probably once larger, for it stood on the crossing of two old roads (from Loders to Nettlecombe, and from Shipton Gorge to Powerstock).

WYTHERSTON

Wytherston lies on the border between the Powerstock Vales and the smaller Hooke Vales and was once in a parish of its own. It cannot be identified with any entry in Domesday Book but from the reign of Henry III to the Dissolution of the Monasteries it belonged to Abbots-

bury Abbey. Hutchins describes it as almost 'depopulated' and the church as 'ruinated long since'. Today it consists of a seventeenth-century farmhouse, some sixteenth-century barns of which the southern end was once the chapel, several cottages and traces of others. Though now isolated, partly by the railway, there is ample evidence that it was once approached by several roads. (See plate 5)

The Hooke Vales (HOV)

STAPLEFORD

Hutchins, writing about the parish of Hooke, remarks that 'Stapleford is supposed to have been the ancient village. But it seems rather to have been a distinct parish long since included in Hooke. Here was anciently a church or chapel.' He also adds that it was granted the right to hold a market and fair in the late thirteenth century. It is perhaps significant that Hooke is divided into two parts, the larger containing the church, and the smaller consisting of farms, mills and Hooke Court. The moated Court was built in about 1400, and it seems probable that this group of buildings marks the site of the old settlement of Stapleford.

The Bride Valley (BRV)

ASHLEY and LOOKE

Although the name Ashley now applies to a farm about a mile-and-a-half south of Long Bredy, and Looke is a large farmstead a mile east of Puncknowle, the two are connected by an old road and have long been closely associated with each other. Lying between the two are the ruins of the ancient Chapel of St Luke, which was partially restored in the mid-1920s when Sir David Milne Watson built a large country house south of Ashley Farm.[8] Settlement remains have been found near the farm, and it seems certain that there was once a hamlet here on the old road between Abbotsbury

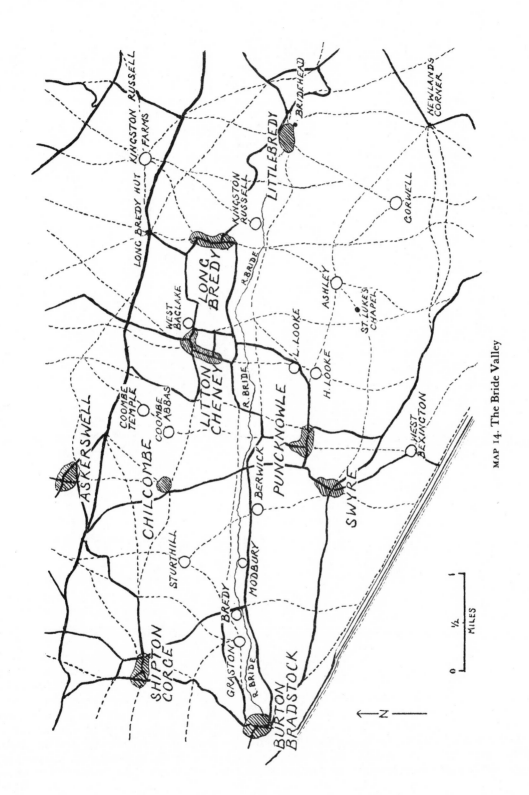

MAP 14. The Bride Valley

Castle and Long Bredy. Looke once comprised two hamlets. One has been demolished in recent years and the other, Looke Farm, is a fine example of a farmstead with an early eighteenth-century farmhouse: it is also perhaps the only place in Dorset where a county road still runs through the actual farmyard. These various facts would seem at first glance to have little connection; but Hutchins states that the Chapel of St Luke once belonged to Ashley and it has recently been suggested that monks from Netley Abbey worked the farm.[9] It seems also to be more than coincidence that the names of Looke and the chapel are so similar. There can be no doubt that further research into the relationship between all three would be valuable. (See map 14)

BREDY

Bredy, or Bonvil's Bredy as it is sometimes called, lies east of Burton Bradstock close to the River Bride. Its history predates the Norman Conquest and according to Hutchins it once had a chapel of ease. It lay in a relatively large manor and though no settlement remains have been recorded it must surely have contained a small settlement. It is now a farmstead standing near a bridge flanking a ford. (See map 14)

GORWELL

Gorwell lies in the parish of Long Bredy about a mile south-west of Ashley and is well documented as a medieval settlement. It is now a farmstead, and the farmhouse itself dates from the sixteenth century. It lies on the old Abbotsbury/Maiden Newton road by way of Wynford Eagle. (See map 14)

GRASTON

Graston lies on a side-stream of the River Bride west of Bredy Farm and is just off the old road from Burton Bradstock to Askerswell. It was once a manor and hamlet, has been identified as part of the Saxon Hundred of Golderonstera, and there is evidence of a medieval settlement near the present buildings. (See map 14)

KINGSTON RUSSELL

Kingston Russell's history goes back to the reign of Edward I, by which time it had acquired the second part of its name and the right to hold a market and fair: but it cannot be distinguished from other Kingstons mentioned in Domesday Book. Not much is known about its later medieval history, but it once had a manor house and a chapel – in ruins by the mid-eighteenth century. Whether the manor house stood near to the chapel or on the site of the existing seventeenth-century Kingston Russell House remains to be determined. Hutchins describes it as a hamlet with some twenty houses, and Taylor's map shows that these stood on the road running south from Long Bredy. Its subsequent history is curious. For various reasons, amongst them enclosure and other changes in agricultural practice, the focus of the parish has shifted to a group of farmsteads north of the present main road (A35) and on the line of its pre-turnpike predecessor, and this cluster of buildings is now called Kingston Russell. The modern farm buildings on the old site are in effect part of Long Bredy, and so Kingston Russell can rightly be regarded as a village which, but for the manor house, has become depopulated, apparently as a result of migration. (See map 14)

The Southern Vales

The Wey Vales (WEV)

WEST BEXINGTON

West Bexington lies behind the Chesil Beach about a mile south of Puncknowle and was once a parish with a chapel dedicated to St

Giles which, according to Hutchins, stood near the sea and had almost disappeared by the eighteenth century. It is said that both village and chapel were burnt by the French in 1430 or 1470 and that the inhabitants were carried away and forced to redeem themselves; since when 'the vill being depopulated it was converted into a farm'. It remained as such until after the First World War when unsuccessful attempts were made to turn it into a seaside resort. Since then it has attracted a number of private residents. (See map 14)

CORTON

Corton is in the parish of Portesham and lies at the foot of a narrow gap at the western end of the Ridgeway. It was once a manor and hamlet and is now a farmstead. The only access is by a steep road through the gap above it, but it once stood on the continuation of the road from Portesham east past the Waddons. Corton is well-known locally, because it claims to contain the smallest church in Dorset. This is slightly misleading because the building is thought to have been a free chapel (*i.e.* one independent of the church of the parish in which it stood). Until its restoration and reconsecration in 1897 it had long been used as a thatched barn. Though Corton was not part of the grant by Cnut to Orc, who founded Abbotsbury Abbey in 1023, its history goes back to before the Norman Conquest.

FRIAR WADDON

Friar Waddon lies half-a-mile north-east of Corton on the other side of Friar Waddon Hill. It seems probable that it originally lay on the north-south road from the Frome valley west of Dorchester to Weymouth. It was held by three thanes prior to the Norman Conquest and at the time of Domesday Book belonged to the religious house of St Mary Villaris in France. Its name suggests that it remained in the hands of the church until after the Reformation, since when it has had a succession of lay owners. It is now a large, but clearly diminished, farmstead with buildings of varied age, including one said to have been a chapel. The farm had the distinction of being amongst the last in Dorset to run a herd of pure-blooded Longhorn cattle, and in order to allow for their immense spread of curving horns some of the byre doors were of an unusual width.

EAST SHILVINGHAMPTON

Lying a mile south of the Waddons, East Shilvinghampton was a hamlet consisting of two farms in Hutchins's time. Settlement remains found adjoining the present buildings indicate that it was once larger.

WEST SHILVINGHAMPTON

This lies less than 400 yards from its companion farmstead and was reduced to a single farm by Hutchins's time. Here again settlement remains suggest it was once larger. Unlike its larger companion it is still served by a county road.

EAST TATTON and WEST TATTON

These lie about a mile from Shilvinghampton on the next ridge south, and Hutchins writes that 'these vills now consist of small farms'. Settlement remains of East Tatton have been reported close to what is now Tatton Farm. Hutchins mentions that West Tatton's farm lay partly in the parish of Portesham and partly in that of Buckland Ripers, but as there are no traces of settlement remains in an appropriate position West Tatton may be a truly 'lost village'. Both places are accounted for in Domesday Book.

SUDDEN

This is a former vill in the parish of Owermoigne now represented by Southdown Farm, which lies at the foot of the hills north of Ringstead Bay. Settlement remains have been recorded south of the farm and there are strip lynchets to the west of it. A fine view of the sites of Sudden, East Ringstead and West Ringstead can be obtained from the down north-east of the farm. (See map 9)

South Purbeck (SP)

Purbeck south of the Hills has a character very much its own, and a character, moreover, which seems to present a clearer picture of the past, especially with regard to the subject of this book, than any other part of Dorset. For this distinctiveness there are many reasons, but four of them are particularly relevant.

First of all Purbeck is not only a peninsula but also nearly an island. It is almost completely divided by a small boggy stream called

Luckford Lake which runs north from East Lulworth across the heath, joining the River Frome opposite Rushton and less than a mile to its east by a second stream which runs north from Povington, joining the Frome at East Holme. Only for a mile or so between East Lulworth and Arish Mell Gap is the peninsula firmly joined to the rest of Dorset. Its isolation is emphasized by the fact that the normal method of entry has traditionally been commanded by the ancient town of Wareham and the adjacent length of the Frome.

Secondly, for many centuries it was controlled on behalf of the Crown by a Governor or Lord-Lieutenant whose rule and law made it virtually independent of the rest of the county. The Governor, whose residence was Corfe Castle, was also given the title of Admiral of the Island.

Thirdly, the whole of Purbeck was a hunting forest from before the Norman Conquest until well into the seventeenth century. Although there is some doubt as to whether it was a hunting forest in the strictest sense of the words or a 'forest, chase and warren', modern historians are of the opinion that it should perhaps be defined as a free warren.[10] Treswell's map of Purbeck, drawn in 1586, shows it as being plentifully stocked with deer except on the limestone plateau of the south-west.

Fourthly, for many centuries South Purbeck has been the home of a vigorous stone-quarrying industry, which still continues. As large-scale building in stone did not begin until after the Norman Conquest and did not reach its height until the early Middle Ages (when the beds of Purbeck marble were exploited), it seems probable that quarrying commenced after Purbeck had become a hunting forest.

South Purbeck's geology has always controlled the distribution of the population. Towards the coast there is a sheltered area of Kimmeridge Clay which extends between Tyneham Gap and Houns-Tout Cliff and on which Kimmeridge village is the only settlement. To the east there is a larger and higher plateau of Jurassic Limestone containing a considerable population scattered along an axis between Worth Matravers and Swanage, itself the centre of the quarrying industry. Between these

two areas and the chalk hills lies a third, and highly relevant, part of Purbeck. This takes the form of a long narrow valley running from Worbarrow Bay to Swanage, and consists of clays and sands of the Wealden series which scarcely occur anywhere else in Dorset. In short a sheltered fertile valley runs like a broad ribbon across Purbeck between the coastal belt and the chalk hills. This valley is watered by the upper branches of the Corfe River; and in early times a small creek ran inland from Swanage for about two miles towards what is now New Barn – it was on the south bank of the creek that Swanage's original settlement stood.

This Wealden valley has for centuries supported a considerable rural population, distributed in such a way as to suggest something unusual in its origin. Excluding Corfe Castle, there is now only one village, Church Knowle, in the whole valley and the rest of the population is distributed in a large number of farms and farmsteads which appear to have originated as small distinct settlements, each with its own block of land. There is evidence that many of these places are smaller than they once were, and in combination they offer more traces of early medieval domestic building than anywhere else in Dorset.

The problems lie in reconciling these farmsteads with the character of a hunting forest and the requirements of the stone industry. Yet it seems certain that all three existed simultaneously. Hutchins suggests that the farmsteads originated as royal hunting lodges and were lived in by the court during the hunting season. That hunting was widespread in the area we know, for there were three forest lodges; one on top of Creech Barrow, another on the shore at Slepe (presumably to control the heath north of the hills), and a third two miles west of Swanage (on 6 OS 1929 this is called Windmill Knap). The difficulty lies in understanding how an area stocked with game could at the same time support an agricultural population. Nevertheless it did so, and that property in the valley was much sought after is indicated by the tenacity with which its landowners clung on to their ancestral acres and added to them whenever possible. One possible explanation is that the houses which Hut-

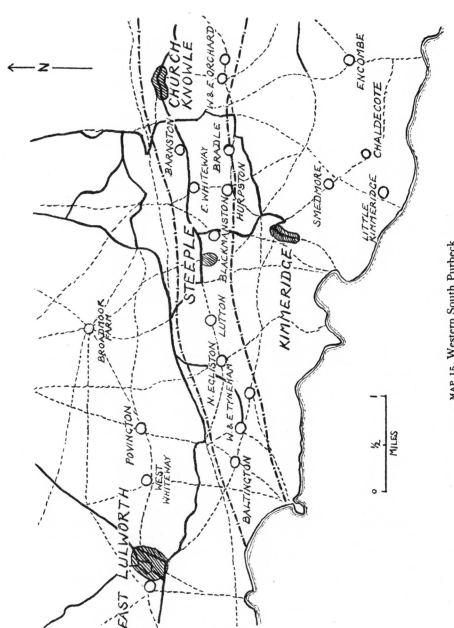

MAP 15. Western South Purbeck

N.B. The thick lines running parallel across the map show the concentration of sites within the Wealden Valley.

chins suggested were hunting lodges (not to be confused with the official forest lodges) were attached to large farms whose tenants cultivated the land and acted as caretakers during the cropping season. This is certainly feasible, for hunting could have continued during the winter without seriously affecting summer activities. If this was the case it would not be unlike the situation in central and southern England during the halycon days of foxhunting in the nineteenth century, when country houses were rented, and sometimes even built, as hunting lodges for use only during the season.

CHALDECOTE

This name has now quite disappeared from maps and its site is confused by the fact that a family of this, or very similar name was once prominent in Purbeck. The present parish of Kimmeridge is covered by two entries in Domesday book, Cameric, the part containing the village; and Cuneliz on the east. The latter was held before the Conquest by Brictuold and after by William de Braiose, and became known as Little Kimmeridge. Hutchins describes three hamlets or farms, Chaldecote, Little Kimmeridge and Smedmore, the first about half a mile east of Smedmore and the second about half a mile south-east of Smedmore, and this accords with Isaac Taylor's map. Hutchins also refers to a farm called Swalland a little east of Chaldecote and in the parish of Corfe Castle, but in the third edition of his *History* the parish of Kimmeridge is described as comprising Great and Little Kimmeridge, Smedmore and Chaldecote. 6 OS 1929 shows Smedmore; Swalland Farm half a mile to the south-east of Smedmore; and a small group of buildings less than half-a-mile due south of Smedmore called Little Kimmeridge. The explanation of all this is to be found on a Smedmore estate map of what is called 'Swalland and Chaldicot Farm' dated 1794/95 which shows that two fields of it, the smaller called Swalland Meadow, were in Corfe Castle parish but the rest, including the buildings called on 6 OS Swalland Farm and Little Kimmeridge, were in Kimmeridge parish. This .state map is very accurate and the field boundaries compare closely with those of 1929. The conclusion most likely is that Chaldecote was

once a small settlement (Hutchins records the ruins of houses there) on the site of which Swalland Farm now stands (see also page 25). (See map 15)

LITTLE KIMMERIDGE

Judging from the conclusion reached about Chaldecote it seems probable that there was once a settlement called Little Kimmeridge or Kimmeridge Parva less than half-a-mile due south of Smedmore. Its site is shown on the estate map dated 1794/5 as a building. This building, or a successor, survived under the name Little Kimmeridge until quite recently. (See map 15)

EASTINGTON

Eastington is a large farmstead lying three-quarters of a mile north-east of Worth Matravers and may be regarded as an example of a group of settlements on the limestone plateau which have either become reduced in size or have been linked with others and lost their individuality. It stands on the ancient 'Priest's Way', the old road linking Swanage with its mother church of Worth. No settlement remains have been recorded, but it was once a manor belonging to Christchurch Priory. (See map 16)

WESTON

Weston lies between Renscombe Farm and Worth Matravers. Settlement remains have been recorded near the Coast Guard Station, itself south of Weston Farm. (See map 16)

Virtually all the farmsteads and farms within the Wealden valley are known to be ancient in origin (most of them are mentioned in Domesday Book), and on the evidence of surviving settlement remains it seems probable that many were larger than they are now. The following are a representative selection:

AFFLINGTON

Afflington, which lies about a mile south-east of Corfe Castle on the old South Valley road, in Hutchins's time was a tithing and farm and he refers to the ruins of buildings there.[11] It was granted the right to hold a market and fair in

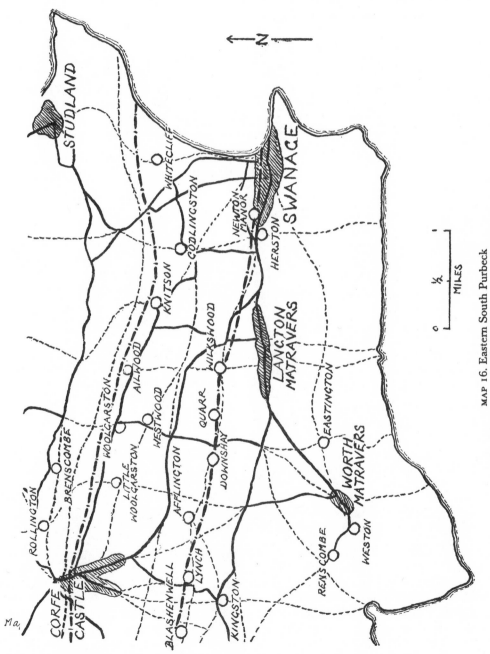

MAP 16. Eastern South Purbeck

N.B. The thick lines running parallel across the map show the concentration of sites within the Wealden Valley.

the reign of Henry III, and it is said that between fifteen and twenty houses still stood there at the end of the seventeenth century. (See map 16)

BARNSTON

Barnston, which lies about half-a-mile west of Church Knowle, contains one of the oldest inhabited houses in Dorset and there are settlement remains nearby. Its name is said to derive from Bern, owner of a house here at the time of Edward the Confessor.[12] The Conqueror bestowed it on Walter de Clavile, descendants of whom still live in the neighbourhood. (See map 15)

BLACKMANSTON

Blackmanston lies 440 yards east of Steeple Church. It has a long history and is associated with many old local families. Settlement remains have been found. (See map 15)

ORCHARD, EAST and WEST

These are south of Church Knowle across the valley stream and must not be confused with the parishes of the same names in North Dorset. Today they are two farmsteads on the old road from Corfe Castle to Kimmeridge. They are less than a quarter of a mile apart and there are settlement remains between them. (See map 15)

WEST TYNEHAM

Though Tyneham is now in ruins and deserted as a result of army occupation, it is surrounded by extensive settlement remains and widespread traces of old cultivation. Treswell's map shows a church with both spire and tower, but confuses the issue by calling this East Tyneham. This latter name belongs to the site of a manor house,[13] about half-a-mile to the east. But whether a settlement was associated with the house remains uncertain. (See map 15)

WHITECLIFF

Whitecliff is the most easterly settlement in the Wealden valley, lying east of Ulwell between Studland Hill and Swanage. Though no settlement remains have been recorded it is men-

tioned in Domesday Book, was once a manor and tithing of Swanage, and is thought to have had a chapel. (See map 16)

EAST WHITEWAY

East Whiteway, or Whiteway, lies between Blackmanston and Barnston and was once a manor and hamlet. It stands on the Corfe Castle/Steeple county road and *RCHM* II reports settlement remains and gives a plan and aerial photograph. West Whiteway is on the heath north of the Purbeck Hills. (See map 15)

On the south side of the Wealden valley on the Upper Purbeck Limestone are a group of settlements closely associated with the Purbeck marble industry.[14, 15] Of these, two may be cited as examples:

DOWNSHAY

Downshay, which lies south of Harman's Cross, is now a hamlet and the old quarry workings can still be seen. Benjamin Jesty, who in 1744 vaccinated his wife with the first smallpox vaccine made from cow-pox, once lived here. (See map 16)

WILKSWOOD

Wilkswood lies on the old South Valley road just within the Wealden in the parish of Langton Matravers. Hutchins, who gives a long account of it, relates that it was once the home of a priory. (See map 16)

On the north side of the valley are a series of settlements near or on the Greensand at the foot of the Purbeck Hills. They all lie on or near the old road from Corfe Castle to Swanage by way of Godlingston. Amongst them is:

LITTLE WOOLGARSTON

This is now a straggle of buildings about a mile east of Corfe Castle. It lies on an old road which ran northward from Winspit to Worth Matravers and was once of considerable importance to the stone industry. Its shape suggests that it was once more concentrated at the southern end. (See map 16)

6

Existing Villages that have Undergone Change

Note on Population Changes

As a result of the agricultural depression of the last quarter of the nineteenth century and the consequent 'drift to the towns', nearly all the rural parishes in Dorset recorded their highest pre-1914 population figures in the mid-nineteenth century. This is clearly shown by the censuses taken between 1801 and 1901.[1] The results of the 1911 census show a further fall and it is clear that the average decline of parish populations at that date was somewhere between forty and fifty per cent. To give a few examples:

Hazlebury
  Bryan dropped from   852 in 1871 to 550 in 1911
Broadwindsor   „   1661 in 1841 to 935   „
Chideock   „   884 in 1851 to 540   „
Corscombe   „   810 in 1841 to 440   „
Maiden Newton „   856 in 1871 to 660   „
Burton
  Bradstock   „   1201 in 1841 to 531   „
Halstock   „   626 in 1841 to 310   „
Cerne Abbas   „   1343 in 1851 to 600   „
Handley   „   1229 in 1851 to 855   „
Piddletrenthide „   860 in 1871 to 540   „

Because of such reductions many villages may be regarded, in the short term, as having suffered loss, and the settlement remains described from them may be no more than the ruins of houses that fell empty in the wake of the depression. To deal with all these would be impossible, but a minority have clearly undergone more radical change, and over a longer period. These latter are best exemplified by about thirty villages scattered throughout the county.

The Poole Basin (PB)

EAST STOKE

Though Hutchins wrongly positioned the village he was correct in saying that 'the in-parish lies scattered over a large common'. He also gives it the alternative names of Stoke St Andrew and Stoke juxta Bindon, the former of which suggests it was the source of the name Lulworth St Andrew (see p. 23), itself once in the parish of East Stoke. The heart of East Stoke shifted across the river when the turnpike road from Wareham to Wool was made. The remains of the ancient church (demolished when the present one was built in 1828) can still be seen in its graveyard, which stands in the meadows about 400 yards south-west of its successor. The ruins stand on a platform which itself looks as if it may have been the site of other buildings.

LYTCHETT MATRAVERS

At the turn of the century the population of this parish was scattered thinly over a broad hill-top, and though there was a slight concentration round The Chequers Inn and at the principal cross-roads most of these buildings were constructed after the making of a branch of the Poole Turnpike Trust which ended at The Chequers. Its history dates back to Domesday Book, and its early history is represented by the parish church, standing isolated from the present village to the west. There are remains of the old village round the church and there is a tradition that it became depopulated by plague, a new settlement growing up later on the supposedly healthier hill-top site to the east.

But as the church was enlarged in about 1400 and extensively rebuilt a century later, it seems possible that depopulation did not take place at the time of the Black Death in 1348. The church dates from the early thirteenth century and contains the tomb of Sir John Matravers (thought to be one of the assassins of Edward II).[2]

WOODSFORD STRANGWAYS

The full name is now obsolete but settlement remains appear to occupy much of the space between what is now called West Woodsford (site of the castle) and East Woodsford where the church and manor house stand. 6 OS 1902 shows the full name in antique lettering and marks the site as north-east of the castle. Whether there was once a single village, of which only the castle, church and manor house now remain, or whether there were two villages – one round the castle and one centred on the church – is still uncertain; but the position of the settlement remains would seem to suggest the former.

The Chalk

The Northern Chalk (NCH)

COMPTON ABBAS

The population of this small parish three miles south of Shaftesbury is divided into two units, now called Compton Abbas and East Compton. These provide a good example of population shift as a result of changes in the local road system. On Isaac Taylor's map East Compton is shown as having a church and being the parish capital; whilst Compton Abbas, with more buildings but no church, has the words 'West Compton up Fields' in subsidiary lettering. Hutchins describes both as a small vill held by Shaftesbury Abbey at the time of Domesday Book. East Compton now consists of little more than a large farmstead. Though the church tower still stands rather forlornly in the middle of its churchyard, Compton Abbas is now the larger settlement. This imbalance was undoubtedly caused by the construction of the turnpike road between Blandford and Shaftesbury through the Iwerne Valley in about 1820. Prior to this few of the villages on its route were joined by main roads and their principal communications tended to run east to west. East Compton was situated on just such a road, but when the turnpike was made communications were re-orientated south to north, a new church was built near the turnpike and the old church at East Compton fell into decay. (See map 17)

HINTON PARVA

This 'little vill ... *alias* Stanbridge' has a puzzling and involved history. Its parish is still so called but its buildings are in two distinct groups; one round the old mill on the River Allen, and the other on the main Wimborne/Cranborne road to the east. The latter is now called Stanbridge and the church there began life as a chapel of Wimborne Minster. The name Stanbridge probably derives from Stone Bridge, which is the name of a bridge three miles further north standing close to Stanbridge Mill.[3] It has been suggested that the chapel was in some way connected with the upkeep of the bridge. There seems no doubt that the original vill was centred round the old mill at Hinton Parva, and it may have had a chapel, later replaced by the Chapel of St Kenelm on the main road. This view is supported by the fact that the lane leading to the mill once ran along the edge of the river to Witchampton. Hutchins mentions that since the chapel had no churchyard the parish buried its dead at Wimborne, but the third edition of his *History* states that 'there is a churchyard at Hinton Parva used as a burial place for the parishioners'.

HORTON

How far it is justifiable to call Horton a lost village remains arguable, but certainly little or nothing survives of the original site except the church, and it is of special interest in the way it illustrates the influences which help to determine the fate of villages. In Saxon times its then lord, Orgar, gave the property to Sherborne Abbey and by the time of Domesday Book there was an abbey or monastery at Horton which, according to Hutchins, was reduced to a cell of Sherborne in 1122. At the time of the Dissolution of the Monasteries Leland records 'This was sumtyme an hedde monastry syns a cell of Sherborne. The village was now a late brent'. Eventually it was sold to Sir Anthony Sturt and inherited by his grandson Humphrey Sturt, whose name constantly recurs among the contemporary landed gentry of Dorset, and who greatly altered the village, rebuilding the manor house and laying out a country estate distinguished by a lake a mile long and an observatory tower. Shortly afterwards Sturt inherited the Crichel estates and abandoned Horton in their favour (see p. 31). The house and grounds declined and the lake disappeared, though its dam can still be seen. At this time the village consisted of little more than the church (said to be the site of the monastery) and the manor house. In 1762 a turnpike road between Ringwood and Horton Inn was made. This, instead of following the old west-east road through the village, which ran by Chalbury Farm, took a more direct line; with the result that a new village arose along it. Today Horton consists almost wholly of post-turnpike buildings, but the church remains to recall the past. It was virtually rebuilt in the early eighteenth century and is notable for two splendid early fourteenth-century monumental effigies.[4] (See map 4)

LANGTON LONG

Langton has been indentified as one of the nine parcels of land bearing the name Bleneford in Domesday Book, of which four, according to Hutchins, subsequently became known as Blandford Forum, Blandford St Mary, Blandford Bryanston and Long Blandford or Langton. He also states that there was once another manor lying between Blandford Forum and Langton and infers that the combination of this with Langton resulted in the latter being called Langton Long Blandford, a name it has long possessed and by which it is still known on 1 OS. The old village of Langton, from which the place derives the first part of its name, scarcely exists as such, but it contains a large medieval church which once boasted a chantry. Hutchins describes the village as almost depopulated, but Isaac Taylor's map does show a small group of cottages centred on the church. He also shows a large house to the south-east of the church. This house was demolished when J. J. Farquharson, one of Dorset's greatest Master of Foxhounds, bought the estate and began to build a new house in 1827. Farquharson's house was itself pulled down in 1949 and several new houses have since been built near its site. The fact that Roman pottery was found on part of the farmstead site in 1840 suggests that the area has known a long history of occupation. (See map 10)

TARRANT CRAWFORD

Tarrant Crawford is now best known as the site of what was once one of the wealthiest Cistercian nunneries in England.[5] The nunnery church has now disappeared and only traces remain of the other buildings. The site is now covered by a large group of farm buildings. The nearby twelfth-century parish church is still in use, and is remarkable for its wall paintings: it is also the burial place of Joanna, Queen of Scotland (daughter of King John) and of Bishop Richard Poore, the guiding force behind the construction of Salisbury Cathedral. The original village is believed to have been in the immediate vicinity of the parish church, but it has since been replaced by a group of buildings near where the old road to Witchampton from Crawford Bridge crosses the Wimborne/Blandford road by way of Shapwick. Settlement remains have been recorded here, but whether the locality merits the name Tarrant Crawford seems uncertain. It is possible that part of the population was moved here; either when the nunnery was at its largest, or after the Dissolution of the Monasteries. There is a direct old road between the two.

The Central Chalk (CCH)

DEWLISH

RCHM records, with a plan, settlement remains over a considerable area called Court Close immediately south of the church.[6] According to Hutchins this included the seat of the Radfords, who probably built it, and was the capital mansion of the manor, but there was also formerly a large house belonging to a Mr Gundry. In due course the estate came to a Mr Michel who built the present Dewlish House, still more to the south, in 1702. It was apparently then that the two older houses were demolished and the park enlarged, and this seems to have involved the diversion westward of the old road from Puddletown from its old line east of the church. (See map 8)

WINTERBORNE CLENSTON

This is still a parish, but if a new church had not been built on the site of an older one in 1849 to meet the needs of the estate, then centred round Whatcombe House, it might, like its neighbours, have faded into oblivion. Although settlement remains have been found at approximately pt. 287 on 1 OS there is now no trace of the original village.[7]

WINTERBORNE WHITECHURCH

Winterborne Whitechurch (also known as Album Monasterium and Blaunch Minster) was once one of a series of closely linked villages on the North Winterborne stream, the little river that joins the Stour at Sturminster Marshall. It stood between two river crossings; that to the north coming from the direction of Cheselbourne, that to the south being part of the pre-turnpike main road between Dorchester and Blandford. The old village lay between these two roads and traces of at least 27 crofts, on both banks of the stream, can be detected. Today this area is vacant and the village consists of two distinct parts; Lower Street in the south, and what is now the village proper on both sides of the Dorchester/Salisbury road (A354). Thus the original south-north axis of the village has changed, mainly because when the Harnham, Blandford and Dorchester Turnpike Trust was formed in about 1750 the new road was made to link up with the cross-roads at the northern end of the village. Once this was done it became inevitable that subsequent building should be along the turnpike. Isaac Taylor's map of 1765 shows no trace of the old village along the stream and it seems probable that its disappearance had taken place at a much earlier date. It is interesting to note that the fourteenth-century parish church once stood in the parish of Milton Abbas, and it may be that prior to becoming a parish church it was an outlying abbey chapelry, ministering to both Winterborne Whitechurch and the other vills in the neighbourhood. (See plate 6)

The Southern Chalk (SCH)

FRAMPTON

Frampton. now a flourishing village on the A37 between Dorchester and Maiden Newton, has changed considerably over the centuries. Domesday Book records it as belonging to the Church of St Stephen of Caen and in due course a priory was established in the village as a cell of Caen Abbey. Frampton Court, built in 1740 and demolished between the First and Second World Wars, stood on the site of the priory. Today Frampton straddles the River Frome and although the two parts do not actually join they were once known as Southover (on the right or south bank of the river) and Northover (on the left or north bank). Today the main road (once a turnpike) runs through Northover, itself the larger of the two settlements. Yet on the south bank, stretching westward for half-a-mile from the site of the old priory, there are settlement remains which have long appeared on maps as 'British settlement' or 'earthworks' but which are probably medieval in origin. Amongst the buildings were a farm, mill and several buildings dating from the seventeenth century, and it seems probable that the settlement remains in Southover belong to the medieval village. The most obvious explanation is that there was once a village, now known as Southover, which became depopulated in the early Middle Ages and was partially rebuilt in the seventeenth century. The church at North-over indicated that there has been a settlement here for at least five hundred years but, unlike the churches in most Dorset villages, there is apparently no masonry older than this in the building. If this is correct then it seems likely that Northover replaced Southover as the site of the heart of the village after alien priories were suppressed in the early fifteenth century. It is worth noting that there are important Roman remains near the river at the north end of Southover.

WEST COMPTON

West Compton lies at the head of a little stream which flows north through Wynford Eagle and is one of the most remote villages and parishes in Dorset. Originally part of King Athelstan's grant to his minster at Milton, it is mentioned in Domesday Book. The population in 1801 was 50; rose to 105 by 1861; and had fallen to 40 by 1911. The 2nd edition of Hutchins remarks 'it is remarkable that not a single farmer or occupier of land resides in the parish. The lands are all annexed to large farms in the adjoining parishes. The inhabitants are all labourers in husbandry numbering . . . 82.'

WHITCOMBE

Whitcombe lies two miles south-east of Dorchester and is one of the best examples in Dorset of a large hamlet. It is still the capital of a small parish and has its own church. Hutchins mentions that it was given by Athelstan to his foundation at Milton and that it remained in the hands of the church until after the Dissolution of the Monasteries, when it passed, with much other property, to the Tregonwells.[8] Today it consists of two parts; a field in which the pleasant towered church stands, and a much larger area in which there is a farmhouse flanked by seventeenth-century barns and a series of cottages arranged round what is almost a village green. The site of the old village is still discernible round the church, in which, incidentally, fragments of a Saxon cross were found early this century. The place is now enclosed on the north and east by a hedge, parts of which have been variously described as covering an 'ancient earthworks' or the traces of a moated manor house.[9] Roman remains have recently been found in the immediate vicinity. (See pl. 7)

The Border Vales – The Northern Vales

The Blackmoor Vale North (BVN)

EAST ORCHARD and HARTGROVE

The parish of East Orchard was formerly a chapelry of Fontmell Magna, and Hartgrove a manor within it containing the chapel. Like Fontmell Magna the area is mentioned in a Saxon charter[10] but the population is now distributed in such a fashion that it is difficult to detect any capital settlement. Former open fields in the south of the parish suggest the existence of a compact village, but the village now survives as a cluster of farms, most of which date from the seventeenth century and which were probably carved out of the old open fields. In the centre of the elongated parish is a scatter of farms and other buildings, all recent, amongst which is the parish church built in 1859 to replace the old Hartgrove chapel which was then demolished. In the north is another modern settlement, New Town, to the east of which is the site of Hartgrove; including both the site of a chapel and a large farmhouse. In the middle of the eighteenth century a country mansion was built at Hartgrove, and the farmhouse, though outwardly modern, probably incorporates part of this mansion. It thus seems probable that there were originally two ancient settlements in the parish, one in the south and one in the north, neither of which survives in a readily recognizable form. (See map 17)

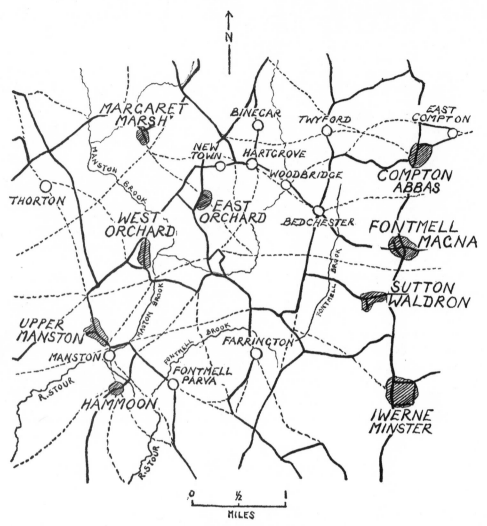

MAP 17. East and West Orchard

SILTON

At the beginning of this century Silton, which lies about a mile south-east of Bourton, was one of the most characteristic lost villages in Dorset, consisting of a parish church and its rectory, and very little else apart from the old manor farm with its outbuildings – amongst which are a tithe barn and a detached range of ox-stalls. Silton remains a parish, but in recent years new houses have been built along Church Road, linking it with the outskirts of Bourton. At the time of the Domesday Survey the manor was held by Edward de Falaise. After the Restoration it was purchased by Sir Hugh Wyndham, commemorated by a fine monument in the church and the survival of an ancient oak tree, under which he liked to sit, in an adjoining field. Through his daughter it became one of the many Dorset properties of Humphrey Sturt. It seems probable that the ancient village was surrounded by open fields, in which case it may have been depopulated when the fields were enclosed, possibly at the date of the Wyndham purchase. The old village seems to have been on both sides of Oxstalls Lane, but for some time 1 OS has ceased to give Silton village status.

TODBER

The parish of Todber, formed in 1434, lies about four miles south of Gillingham. Of less than 400 acres it is one of the smallest in the county, and is completely enclosed by its two much larger neighbours, Marnhull and Stour Provost. Of the medieval settlement only the chapel (once a chapelry of Gillingham and almost entirely rebuilt in 1879) survives and there are no signs of any ancient buildings in its immediate vicinity. Nevertheless, it is mentioned in Domesday Book and several worked stones belonging to a Saxon churchyard cross were found during the rebuilding of the chapel.[11] At one time it was held by William de Moione and the place-name Moigne or Moyne, found in several parts of Dorset, derives from his family. Much of Todber and the most of Stour Provost was once open common. Enclosure of this began early, perhaps in the thirteenth century, and the process continued on until a final division of farms and fields took place in the late eighteenth century. It was then that new and straight enclosure roads, now so prominent, were made and cottages built along them. It may be supposed that these cottages (some of which remain in Shave Lane) were erected to house at least part of the population of the old village, which Taylor's map suggests stood near the church. Indeed, there is still a disused well-house here containing a pump which until well into this century supplied the local inhabitants with water. At the beginning of this century the church was flanked by quarries, and it may be that part of the original site has been destroyed by these workings. (See pl. 8)

The Blackmoor Vale West (BVW)

BELCHALWELL

Belchalwell, which lies north-east of Woolland, is no longer a parish, having been absorbed into those of Fifehead Neville and Okeford Fitzpaine; but in Hutchins's time it was a small parish, to which he gives the alternative names of 'Belle in le Downes' and 'Belle', and his further remarks suggest that Belle and Chalwell might once have been two separate places. Today Belchalwell is a ghost of a village with a charmingly situated church in whose roof bees have long nested; but about half-a-mile south-east, on the old road between Shaftesbury and Dorchester, is a group of buildings called Belchalwell Street which show traces of seventeenth-century construction.

EAST CHELBOROUGH
and LEWCOMBE

East Chelborough, which is mentioned in Domesday Book, consists almost entirely of two separate farms on the road from Red Post to Yeovil and has a long history, best expressed by what appear to be the sites of two medieval castles, one with a motte and bailey. It has obviously undergone great change, because the church at Lewcombe, nearly a mile away, is now the parish church. This building, said to have been built in the sixteenth century on the site of a twelfth-century chapel, lies together with the seventeenth-century manor house in the extreme north of the present parish of East Chelborough. It thus seems probable that East Chelborough itself, in which there are no buildings earlier than 1600, has no fundamental connection with Lewcombe, and that the small settlement round the castle disappeared in the Middle Ages. This in turn suggests that when part of the site was reoccupied, perhaps in the wake of local land enclosures, the parish boundaries were extended to include Lewcombe Church, the vill of which had also been abandoned.

FOLKE

The old capital settlement of this parish lies some two and a half miles south-east of Sherborne

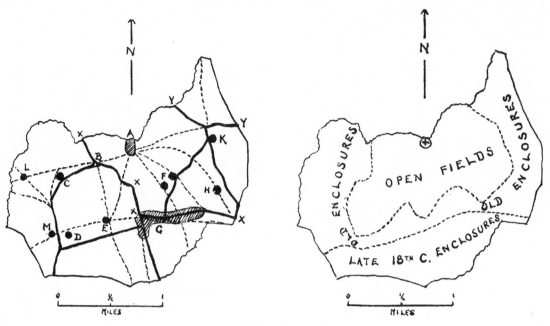

MAP 18. The Parish of Holwell

KEY

County roads are shown as a continuous line
Old roads and tracks are shown as a broken line

A Holwell Village (the Borough) and church
B Barnes Cross
C Buckshaw
D Holwell Manor
E Westrow
F Hill Street

G Area of Population concentration now replacing the old village
H Piccadilly
K Woodbridge
L Lower Buckshaw
M Sandhills
X Part of the old Blandford–Sherborne turnpike over Bulbarrow
Y Part of the old Blandford–Sherborne turnpike through Bishop's Caundle

and is now one of the most remote in the Blackmore Vale, consisting only of the church, a Jacobean manor house and a handful of other buildings. The church was extensively rebuilt and enlarged in 1628, and later a new northern entrance was made to replace the old south porch.[12] This suggests that the population gradually migrated north and that this move was accelerated at a later time by the making of the turnpike road between Sherborne and Blandford, which runs through the hamlet of Allweston. This is supported by the statement in the third edition of Hutchins that Allweston for-

merly contained 10 houses but by 1871 contained 50, and by census figures which show that the parish population rose from under 200 in 1801 to over 300 in 1861.

HOLWELL

The parish of Holwell lies in the middle of the Blackmoor Vale about fifteen miles north of Dorchester and, perhaps because until 1844 it formed a detached part of Somerset, remains one of the less familiar.[13] The capital settlement, with it handsome church and list of incumbents going back to 1301, stands on the

Caundle Brook in the middle of the northern boundary, but it is now only approachable by a blind lane from Barnes Cross some half-a-mile to the west. Even a century ago, when the population of most Dorset villages was at its highest, it was described as home for a mere six or seven families. Though the figure cannot greatly have increased since it was once much larger, a fact proved by both the size of the church and the fact that part of it has long been called The Borough, though the exact significance of this name is now lost. The parish also contained the principal lodge of the Forest of Blackmoor, described by Leland as having been deforested during the reign of William the Conquerer despite the fact that there is plenty of evidence to suggest it continued to exist until much later. During the Middle Ages it was surrounded – as far as the course of the Brook permitted – by open fields covering almost half the parish. Though it is thought that these were enclosed no later than the sixteenth century, the existing pattern of the fields is reminiscent of much later enclosures. Finally, the southern part of the parish was once part of the great common which stretched into the parishes of Pulham, Glanvilles Wootton and Mappowder. Across this, roughly along the line of its border with the cultivated fields, ran a rough track westward from Kingstag. In 1796 the common was enclosed by Act of Parliament and a new, hedged road laid across it. East of Crouch Hill this followed the line of its predecessor, but further west it took a new course to the south of the old road. This western part, though only a mile long, is a good example of an enclosure road running over former common land, for its wide verges were intended as a substitute for the rights of grazing over the common held previously by the cottagers in the area. These changes are reflected in the distribution of the parish population today. Round the rim of the old open fields lie a series of small settlements; namely Buckshaw Farm, Buckshaw itself (once the property of Sherborne Abbey), Sandhills, Westrow, Hill Street (among whose houses is the fourteenth-century Naish Farm), and finally another group of farms, a little to the east, part of which is known somewhat unexpectedly by the name Piccadilly. The position of these

settlements suggested that they once lay on the edge of the open fields and that when land further to the west and east was enclosed they drew population away from the old village of Holwell, which henceforth ceased to be the centre of the open field system. Thus the enclosures of 1796 and the making of a turnpike between Blandford and Sherborne at about the same time[14] had the usual effect of drawing new building towards the new road, since when ribbon development has taken place at Packers Hill, Pleck and Crouch Hill, where today the bulk of the population lives, and includes post office, chapel and village hall – with the result that this has become the new 'village of Holwell'. (See map 18)

NORTH WOOTTON

North Wootton lies about two miles south-east of Sherborne and is yet another example of migration towards a turnpike road. The old medieval church, round which settlement remains are still visible, is about 400 yards north of the present main road on which its replacement stands. Except for the tower it was demolished when the latter was built in 1883. (See map 11)

Trans-Yeo (TY)

ADBER

This is no longer a village in the strict sense of the word, being part of the parish of Trent, but there are hints that it may once have been one. Trent was transferred to Dorset at the end of the last century, and Adber itself affords a striking example of the way in which road and rail may alter the nature of a settlement.[15] Adber was held by the Earl of Mortain at the date of the Domesday Survey and by 1930 consisted of numerous scattered farm buildings, many of them surrounded by orchards. That Adber was once larger is suggested by the site of a church (the Chapel of St Mary), said never to have recovered from damage suffered in the Civil War; whilst the remains of a fifteenth-century churchyard cross (recently re-erected in a more prominent position) suggest that it once had its own burial ground. At least six of the farm buildings show traces of seventeenth-century contruction. Adber is now a back-water and *cul-de-sac* lying in a triangle formed by the B3148; part of the road between Ilchester and Sandford Cross through Adber Cross; and by the old Great Western Railway on the west. It is particularly rich in old tracks and footpaths and what must have been the village street is clearly the stub of the old road from Nether Compton to Marston Magna. (See map 12 and plate 9)

The Border Vales – The Western Vales

MAPPERTON

This name occurs as that of an old hamlet in the parish of Sturminster Marshall and, with several variants, in an area about two miles south-east of Beaminster. Both are mentioned in Domesday Book, but it is the latter with which we are concerned. I OS attaches the name to a settlement which includes Mapperton Manor and Mapperton Farm, three-quarters of a mile to the west. But Hutchins mentions two distinct places; North Mapperton in the parish of Beaminster, which he describes as 'anciently a manor', and South Mapperton, a parish of its own. North Mapperton is now represented by Marsh Farm, and the old village of South Mapperton seems to have been situated in the vicinity of the parish church and old manor house. It seems that the entire parish was depopulated by the plague in 1666. At that time Mapperton churchyard was unconsecrated and its inhabitants were traditionally buried in Netherbury, but when the plague struck the villagers refused to allow Mapperton's plague victims to be buried in Netherbury for fear of infection.[16] It was therefore arranged that the bodies should be left on the parish boundary and later removed for burial to the top of South Warren Hill, itself inside the parish of Netherbury but far from any dwellings. The bodies were left where the old Mapperton/Netherbury road crosses the parish boundary. The spot is now marked by a tree called the Posy or Cosy Tree, and the name 'Posy' may derive from the common practice of carrying posies of flowers and herbs to ward off the infectious humours thought to carry the plague. There is still a small enclosure on the windswept summit of South Warren Hill which is said to mark the burial place of the plague victims, and bones have been disinterred there.

MELPLASH

West and East Melplash were originally two small settlements in the parish of Netherbury, and both have virtually disappeared. West Melplash, described by Hutchins as 'once a manor but now a hamlet of ten houses', survives as an old house, Melplash Court, but no hamlet remains have yet been found. East Melplash, also known as Barbridge, was originally half-a-mile north-east in a little valley leading towards Mapperton. The decay of East and West Melplash was caused by the construction of the Bridport/Beaminster turnpike along a diversion away from Melplash Court and between the two hamlets. Subsequent building took place along the new road and it is this that now constitutes the village of Melplash.

STANTON ST GABRIEL

Despite its position on the edge of the sea south of Morcombelake, Stanton St Gabriel is one of the better-known shrunken, and indeed almost lost, villages in Dorset. It is still a parish with one or two houses and the ruins of its church. The existing Chapel of St Gabriel, built in 1841, stands on the old road between Bridport and Lyme Regis – later a turnpike. Stanton St Gabriel seems therefore to be a typical example of population migration from what was probably a small fishing village in a sheltered site close to the sea to a more accessible position further inland.

The Border Vales – The Southern Vales

BUCKLAND RIPERS

This small village in the parish of Chickerell lies on a tiny stream in a narrow lateral valley of the Wey and is still one of the most secluded villages in the county, despite its proximity to Weymouth. Apart from a few modern buildings it now consists of the church, manor house and Buckland Farm, but there are settlement remains both east and west of the church, indicating that it was once larger. It was probably at its largest when, before the union of Weymouth and Melcombe Regis, it stood on a direct road north from Weymouth, and its decline is likely to have commenced when the building of a bridge between the two towns helped to concentrate the approach to both through Melcombe Regis. According to Hutchins both church and manor house were burnt in 1655; this too may have had some effect on the village.

EAST FLEET

East Fleet is perhaps best known today as the setting for the title of Meade Falkner's book *Moonfleet*, and this, together with its proximity to Weymouth, has made it one of the most familiar shrunken villages in the county. It is also unique in being the only village in the county to have been destroyed by the sea, for the old village, which lay in a little indentation on the landward side of the Fleet, was largely destroyed in 1824 when the sea broke through Chesil Beach and swamped it.[17, 18] The old church was badly damaged and only the chancel now survives. A new church was later built on higher ground nearby.

RADIPOLE

Radipole's long history derives from its position at a point where the River Wey broadens out into Radipole Lake, before entering the harbour passage and reaching the sea. It seems possible that the village once stood at the head of a comparatively broad estuary, for Melcombe Regis stands on a spit of shingle and sand which may well have lengthened considerably over the last two thousand years. If this is so then it seems probable that the Roman port of Clavinium occupied Radipole's site, and Radipole itself may have been a port until the movement of Lodmoor Beach led to silting up of the approach to it. By the date of the Domesday Survey Radipole belonged to the church and in the early Middle Ages the village lay on the eastern edge of its own large parish. For centuries its church was the mother-church of the settlement of Melcombe, and it was not until 1600 that their roles were reversed. Today all that remains of the medieval village is a small thirteenth-century church and a manor house, but a large six acre field deeply carved into mounds and hollows which lies west of the church and is known locally as Humpty Dumpty Field probably marks its original site. Amongst the hollows is one which runs the length of the field and then forks, one branch heading towards Radipole Lake and the other running west as if to join the old road from Radipole to Weymouth. The field is unlike most reputed medieval village sites in that it lies on a marked slope and the 50 foot contour runs across the middle of it. The position and character of the site suggest that it was the site of Roman Clavinium and it would be of interest to know whether any Roman remains have been found in the field. The date of the abandonment of the settlement is not known, but it probably was caused by the growth of Melcombe Regis[19] and it is possible that plague may have played a part. During the nineteenth century houses were built along the road from the church towards Wyke Regis, especially near a mill on the river, and these gradually replaced those of the abandoned village. Since 1900 Radipole has been gradually absorbed into Weymouth.

Villages Submerged by Modern Buildings and other Place Names not Precisely Identified

The preceding chapters have been concerned with old settlements whose sites and names are well enough known to enable them to be considered in something like logical sequence, and there now remain to be mentioned a number of place-names whose locations are at least uncertain and in most cases unknown. It is further enquiry into these which is most likely to add to our knowledge of Dorset's lost villages.

Most of these names are best taken in alphabetical order but it is first convenient to recall that a number of old places have become submerged by the spreading tide of urban development. This is particularly noticeable in the Wey Vales where the spread of Weymouth has over-run at least two old hamlets, EAST CHICKERELL and PUTTON, both of which were once manors. The former was a large farmstead as late as 1930, and the latter which stood about quarter of a mile east of the old village of Chickerell, now gives its name to a much wider area of suburb.

Here too were the places referred to by Hutchins in the following words:[1]

'N.B. On the river Wey are the following eight vills, which take their name from it, mentioned in ancient records, and still existing except the last two; Upway or Way St Laurence, Broadway or Way St Michael's, St Nicholas, Stottingway, Crecketway, Causeway, Way Riward and Rowald's Way.'

All these are now part of Weymouth or, if not actually submerged in it, are joined to it by building. The first still exists as the village of Upwey; the second and third are in Broadwey and are probably one and the same (the ori-ginal dedication of the church was to St Michael but it was changed to St Nicholas in 1402); the fourth survives in Broadwey as the name of a road (perhaps an indication of its site); the fifth was once a manor and later a farm; and the final three are probably three different names for one and the same place (one name still survives in that of Causeway Farm near Radipole).[2]

Rather similarly HERSTON and the old manor of NEWTON have been swallowed up by Swanage.[3] WESTPORT was once a hamlet standing just outside Wareham's west gate, but by the eighteenth century had only one house (it was later the site of a turnpike gate and is now part of the suburb on the Worgret Road). BESTWALL, on the opposite side of Wareham, was in a relatively similar position. LEIGH was once a manor, hamlet and tithing on the east side of Wimborne and though now joined to the town still survives. DUDSBURY, in West Parley, is probably one of several old places to have been over-run by the growth of Bournemouth. MIDDLESTREET was, as its name implies, the central of three distinct settlements now merged to form the village of Spetisbury.[4] LANGCOTES, or Winfrith Langcotes, was described by Hutchins as 'in Winfrith a little north-east of the church' and may have been that part of the present village south of the pre-turnpike road which ran across the middle of the village and of which School Lane is part. WYKE, lies due west of Gillingham and is now a ribbon suburb on the Shaftesbury/Wincanton road. It is erroneously described by Hutchins as 'a hamlet situated a mile north-west of Gillingham'.

Place-names not Precisely Identified

AILWEL

This is one of two names given in the first edition of Hutchins to a farm in Frome St Quintin 'where anciently there was a chapel'. His third edition spells the word Oileywell, surely a version of Holywell, the name now associated with buildings at Evershot railway station. If, as the name suggests, the well had religious associations, it is quite likely that there was a chapel there. The exact site of the 'holy well' is difficult to place because the whole area abounds in springs issuing from the Chalk at its junction with the Greensand, and is now much built over; but it seems probable that it lay just west of Horchester in the parish of Frome St Quintin where a spring is shown on 6 OS 1903 300 yards south-south-west of Evershot railway station and just north of Burl Farm.

BAGGERIDGE

Though the name is not shown on Isaac Taylor's map Hutchins mentions that 'Baggeridge or Baggeridge Street' was once a hamlet. Despite the fact that no settlement remains have been recorded it has been suggested that the hamlet may have been near Bagman's Coppice, on what is now called Knowle Hill, Woodlands.[5] (See map 4)

BAGLAKE

This name survives in that of Baglake Farm which, though in Long Bredy, is in effect the easternmost building in Litton Cheney. Hutchins gives the name East Baglake as one of the names for Dowerfield which lay between West Baglake and Long Bredy. No traces of settlements survive and it has been suggested that the Dowerfield and Baglake of today originated as moves from an earlier site.[6] (See map 14)

BESTEDON

This is referred to by Hutchins as an unknown place in Cattistock, but it does not appear on Isaac Taylor's map and nothing else seems to be known about it.

BLACKLAND

This is said to be the name of a parcel of land in the parish of Lydlinch.

BLANDFORD MARTEL

This is thought to be the correct name for the cluster of houses opposite the entrance gate to Bryanston School and now in the parish of Blandford St Mary. (See map 10)

BROUNSELL

Hutchins describes Brounsell Lane as a small hamlet near Caundle Wake 'in former ages considerable enough to give name to a Hundred'. The only remaining trace of the name is Brounsell Knap, a short steep rise in the road between Lydlinch and Purse Caundle. On 6 OS 1930 the name is applied to a sharp bend in the road near where are shown some small buildings, and this may mark the site of the original settlement.

BURTON

This name (common in Dorset) is given by Hutchins to one of the three tithings of Marnhull and may have been one of the original settlements in the parish. It is apparently only known from a *terrier* of an Abbot of Glastonbury in the early sixteenth century.

CALDWELL

This name is equated by Hutchins with that of Ailwel (see above), but there is no trace of the name in this region on modern maps, and a careful reading of pp. 504, 505 in the first volume of Hutchins's first edition, and also his account of Belchalwell (see p. 65 above) suggests that he may have been confused between Frome St Quintin and Fifehead St Quintin and that the name Caldwell relates to the latter rather than the former and is therefore not near Ailwel.

CORINGDON

Coringdon is described by Hutchins as 'once a hamlet now only a farm with two or three cottages at the foot of the N. hill a little S.W. of Studland'. This suggests that it stood on the present Swanage/Studland county road at a point about level with Forked Down End. The situation is complicated because in 1860 the old road north from Jenny Gould's Gate, which ran over what is now the golf course, was closed and a new road was made in a more north-westerly direction. Currendon Farm (presumably a version of Coringdon) stands on the new road, and it seems possible that the hamlet was finally demolished when the farm was built. Coringdon is also the name of a manor in the parish of Corscombe said to have had a chapel and to have belonged to Sherborne Abbey. It may have been sited near Corscombe Court.

CROCKERN STOKE and STOKE TURBERVILLE

Careful reading of Hutchins seems to suggest that these were two hamlets in the parish of Hazelbury Bryan.[7] Further support for this view comes from the fact that Stoke Wake is the village nearest to Hazelbury Bryan and that both villages were involved in the enclosure of Stoke Common. Hazelbury Bryan is today unusual in being made up of five more or less distinct centres (Droop, Pidney, Kingston, Wonston and Woodrow) and it may be that Crockern Stoke and Stoke Turberville are earlier names for two of these.

DOWN

This name gains a passing reference in Hutchins as that of one of two scattered hamlets (the other being Marsh, q.v.) south-west of Bishop's Caundle, and it seems that the buildings now comprising Bishop's Down include both hamlets. (See map 11)

EARNLEY

This is probably the original name of a manor in the eastern part of the parish of Corscombe now known as Benville. The change in names took place between 1436 and 1539.[8]

FORESHILL

This is the name of two old manors near Winfrith today represented by West and East Fossil

Farms. The land associated with West Foreshill probably contained a small settlement which is mentioned in the Bindon Abbey charter of 1313.[9] (See map 9)

FROME

Hutchins gives the name to a place 'now swallowed up in Woodlands' north of Wimborne which owed its name to a family from Frome in Somerset.

FROME PANTERS

Frome Panters is said to have been in the manor of Frome Whitfield and 'near the boundary of Stinsford', but there is no indication of its status and it is not shown on Isaac Taylor's map. It is interesting to note however that until recently there was a small building called Painters Barn in an appropriate position a little west of the road from Dorchester to Piddlehinton, at the north end of a farm road still shown on 1 OS as running from Coker's Frome.

GUMMERSEY or GOMERSHAY

Hutchins uses the second spelling and describes it as west of Stalbridge, whilst Isaac Taylor shows Gummersey east of Stalbridge and Gomershay to its south. Today 1 OS shows Gomershay Farm on the Bibbern Brook and close to the River Stour. (See map 6)

HAMSTEAD

Hamstead seems to have been a settlement in the neighbourhood of Lulworth. It would appear to have been nearer East than West Lulworth, but it is perhaps worth noting that the name Hambury is well known in the latter.[10]

HIDE

Hutchins includes seven places with this name in his index (in Bothenhampton, Bere Regis, Frampton, Lydlinch, Puddletown, Sherborne and Steeple) and it seems likely that there were others. It has been suggested that Hide was a hamlet at Waterston in Puddletown and there is the site of a medieval settlement to the west of Lower Waterston House, but it has also been suggested that Hide was where Druce Farm now is.[11]

HORSYCH

Hutchins describes this as a hamlet in the parish of Cranborne with a history dating back to 1332.[12] Fägersten mentions it as being in the 'old and much larger parish of Cranborne' and it has been equated with Eastworth Farm in the parish of Verwood, itself carved out of the parish of Cranborne in the late nineteenth century. A recently drawn map has placed it on the north side of a sharp bend in the River Crane just north of Redman's Hill in the parish of Horton.[13]

HYDE

Hutchins calls this place Hyde juxta Pimperne and describes it as a manor and hamlet in Tarrant Hinton but 'so near to Blandford and Pimperne that some parcels of it belonged to the town'. Until 1933 a tongue of Tarrant Hinton ran west as far as the A354 and, as the name Hyde still survives here in the name of a farm, it seems probable that Hyde was somewhere in this area of the parish. A manorial map gives the name La Hyd and shows it as adjoining Pimperne.[14]

KENTLEWORTH

Hutchins quotes an old document that refers to Kentleworth as 'now called Marnhulle'. He also suggests that it may have been the part of Marnhull round Yardgrove Farm.

KNOLL (A)

Hutchins describes this as 'once a manor and hamlet but now only two grounds' in East Lulworth. It is not shown on Taylor's map but 6 OS 1902 marks a patch of partly wooded ground half-a-mile south east of the village called Boat Knoll.

KNOLL (B)

This was once a member of the manor of Buckland Newton, but if there was a settlement it has either changed its name or completely disappeared. It has been identified with Henley, an outlying part of Buckland Newton, but 1 OS only applies the name to a hill east of the village.

LANGEFORD

It is probable that this name, mentioned in Domesday Book, refers to a medieval settlement called Rushton or Ruston, now represented by St Leonard's Farm in the extreme south-west of the parish of West Moors. It has been suggested that the name derives from that of a ford which preceded Palmer's Bridge over the Moors River.[15]

LASTOCK

Hutchins describes this as one of the hamlets of Netherbury and as being three miles south-west of Stoke Abbott. This would place it in the centre of the Marshwood Vale, where the names Wild Stoke, Stoke Mill and Stoke Mill Lane all survive. It has also been associated with the manor of Bromlegh, in which case it may refer to what is now Laverstock Farm about half-a-mile south-west of Brimbley Coombe Farms.

LESTIFORD

This name has been identified with a member of the Saxon Hundred of Cranborne and the names Levetisford and Levetsford are both included in Hutchins Index to Domesday Book. It has been suggested that the name applies to a ford near Verwood and a map has placed it on the River Crane at a point due east of the south-east corner of Birches Copse.[16]

LITTLE CRICHEL

This is one of the two original settlements of Moor Crichel or Crichel Magna. There is no longer any sign of the village, but it is thought to have been situated between Moor Crichel and Long Crichel near Norwood Farm. The manor and its old house were purchased from the Okedens in 1868 and incorporated into the Sturt estates. (See map 4)

MARSH

See Down.

NETHERSTOKE

Though this is thought to have been a manor and hamlet with a chapel belonging to Sherborne Abbey, it is now a scatter of buildings lying on the road between Halstock and Yeovil. It is mentioned by name in a Saxon charter[17] and Hutchins mentions a field called Chapel Close as being near the county boundary north of Halstock church.

NEWNHAM

This was described by Hutchins as a farm in Stalbridge but it has recently been suggested that it belongs to the site of an old settlement now marked by buildings called Newnham on a tithe map dated 1839.[18] These are 400 yards south of Ryall's Farm where 6 OS shows some unnamed buildings. (See map 6)

NEWTON

The name here applies to a 'new' town planned by Edward I in 1286 at the base of the Goathorn Peninsula on the heathland north of Studland. It seems that the King intended to found a port to rival Poole, but it is doubtful whether any actual building was done, or if it was, whether any traces remain. It is perhaps significant that 1 OS 1960 shows the name in a position about half-a-mile north-west of Greenland, and this may well be near the site of the original settlement.[19]

RAMSBURY

This lost name is attached by Hutchins to a manor and small farm now in the parish of Lydlinch. Isaac Taylor writes the name across a tract of land on the west side of the River Lydden, but it has been suggested that Berry Farm, on the east of the stream, is the most likely modern representative.[20] (See map 6)

ROTHERSDENE

This name is shown on Thomas Ailwell's map of Cranborne Chase (1618) as just south of Harbin's Park, but no other reference to it has been recorded.[21] This would have been a likely site for a settlement, at the crossing of the Pimperne/Shaftesbury road and the road from Child Okeford to Tarrant Gunville.

SELAVESTONE

Nothing seems to be known about the locality of the name, but Hutchins does give Alveston as an alternative name for Allweston near Sherborne.

SPUTEL

Sputel was once a farm in Beer Hackett belonging to the Knights Hospitallers, from whom the name presumably derives, but there is no trace of it on 6 OS.

STOKE TURBERVILLE

See Crockern Stoke.

SYDLING FIFEHEAD

This has been mentioned in connection with Sydling St Nicholas but no indication of its exact position has yet been recorded.[22]

TARRANT ANTIOCH

It seems probable that Tarrant Antioch and Tarrant Rawston were two closely associated vills in the lesser valleys of the Chalk. Settlement remains have been recorded south of Tarrant Rawston and these may well indicate its site.

TOLLERFORD

This the name of an old Hundred and once applied to a piece of ground 'at the centre of four crossways' a little north of Maiden Newton on the road to Little Toller. There was an ironworks there at the beginning of the present century.

TOTCOMBE

This is the name of an old Hundred whose court was held in a small valley 'W. of the great road from Sherborne to Dorchester near the bounds of Cerne and Nether Cerne'. It has been suggested that it was once a village sited in Bramble Bottom near Totcombe Wood.[23]

UGGESCOMB

This is also the name of a Hundred and according to Hutchins it belongs to a small valley formed by Hampton and Ridge Hills north of Portesham, 'now called Mystecomb'. 6 OS 1903 places Black Down Barn there, about 750 yards due south of the Hardy Monument, but it is not now named on 1 OS.

UPHILL

According to Hutchins this name applies only to land in the parish of Coombe Keynes, but it has been suggested that this land, to the east of the village, was the site of the lost village of Uphill.[24] Unless represented by the few buildings at Kimbert's End it is now quite deserted.

WESTWOOD

At the end of the eighteenth century Westwood was a farm in Coombe Keynes and Isaac Taylor's map shows it in the position now occupied by Westwood Coppice. It has been suggested that it was once a village, in which case both it and the farm have completely disappeared.[25]

WHITSTOW

Taylor's map of 1765 shows this name as that of a little hamlet in what afterwards became the park of Canford House near Wimborne.

The actual site is a piece of uneven ground in and near a group of trees at a junction of tracks. There is a modern barn there now, and it is said that ancient drains were exposed when the barn was built.

YEWSTOCK

This name is now associated with two houses on the B3092 near the boundary between Sturminster Newton and Hinton St Mary, at a point where there was once a turnpike gate belonging to the Vale of Blackmore Trust.[26]

In addition to all these place-names Fägersten (*op. cit.*) mentions some twenty-five others which he describes as 'lost'.

8

The Causes of Desertion and Shrinkage

The potential causes of the desertion and shrinkage of villages all but rival the number of settlements themselves and it is probably true to say that in no two cases have these causes been exactly the same. Nor are the reasons always clear, and in some, notably among the truly deserted villages, they are unlikely ever to be fully understood.

It is first worth noting that a high proportion of the more obviously lost and shrunken villages are situated on the Chalk and that of these half are sited in or close to river valleys. The one inch maps of the Geological Survey show that in nearly all the valleys of the Chalk, especially in the north, deposits of now dry valley gravels reach to points considerably above the present sources of streams. This appears to indicate a gradual lowering of the water table, whilst the absence of settlements above the present sources suggests that the reduction may be due to climatic changes which took place long before the valleys were settled by the Saxons. It is important to remember that the availability of water must always have been a prime factor in the choice of village sites, and there are many localities, both on and off the Chalk (*e.g.* Weston in Corscombe and Bonscombe in Shipton Gorge) that appear suitable for settlement on this account though no remains of villages have yet been reported.

In comparison with the Chalk the comparable number of deserted sites in the Northern Vales are few and little is known about most of them. Their scarcity in the Blackmoor Vale North may be ascribed to the fact that the Forest of Gillingham survived in some form until well into the seventeenth century, and that for the most part enclosure took place at a later

date.[1] Elsewhere the Blackmoor Vale was once extensively covered by the Forest of Blackmore,[2] and here the outstanding site is Colber, a deserted medieval village near Sturminster Newton.

The number of deserted sites in the Western Vales (except those in the Bride Valley) is also small, a fact which would seem to indicate an unusually high resistance to change. The soils in the Marshwood Vales are almost wholly derived from the Lias and it seems that, until this century, the area has known less movement of population than anywhere else in the county and has long supported the maximum numbers it could reasonably accommodate.

A very different picture is presented by the Southern Vales, and the number of deserted sites along the coast is high. Those in the Wey Vales are now mostly obscured by the growth of Weymouth, but they offer evidence of a feature common throughout the county; namely the concentration of many small settlements in short valleys (in this case that of the River Wey). The special situation in the Wealden Valley in South Purbeck has already been noted, but there are about half-a-dozen sites on the limestone plateau to its south, and it would be of value to learn more about the relationship between their distribution and the history of the Forest of Purbeck.

The emphasis which has been put upon the connexion between the old villages and the Chalk and other calcareous soils is due to the fact that the latter have long provided the county with much of its arable farmland. There is much evidence to suggest that the majority of these settlements depended on the open field system, and that when these fields were enclosed or broken up into farms the disruption that followed led to the desertion and shrinkage of many of the villages themselves. It is worth remembering that the enclosure of the open fields was eventually reinforced by the enclosure of much of the 'waste' and 'common', and as both were not entirely without settlement it seems safe to claim that enclosure, in its broadest sense, had a major influence on the fate of many villages and settlements.

Apart from enclosure the factor which seems most closely associated with changes in the distribution of the rural population is that of changes in the local road traffic pattern, of which the most important was the coming into Dorset of the turnpike system in about 1750.[3]

It is reasonable to assume that prior to the Norman Conquest 'ways' of one sort or another ran in all directions between neighbouring villages. This system of traffic routes may be likened to a mesh net in which the villages were the nodes and the ways between them the strings. A network of this kind was eminently suited to an age when vehicles were few and all movement was by horse or foot, and in recent years its size has been revealed by the 'way-marking' of bridle roads and footpaths. Though the redistribution of the population made sections of this network obsolete its overall pattern remained much the same until after the Civil Wars, and what remains of it is still faintly visible in our modern road system. The effect of changes in the road system on Dorset's lost and shrunken villages cannot be overestimated. Many sites are to be found on roads now redundant and, perhaps more important for the investigator, the course of old roads often provide clues as to the whereabouts of old settlements.

A glance at the 1 inch Ordnance Maps (1 OS) shows that the basis of the modern road system, namely that formed by the coloured 'county' roads, is still a network, but one of quite astonishing irregularity. In places too it is highly illogical, for there are large tracts of country across which no road in the modern sense now runs. The main reason for these changes was undoubtedly the gradual introduction of the turnpike system.

The coming of the turnpikes had three effects. First, as they were better built than any of their predecessors they gradually canalized the traffic, especially as vehicles became more numerous and comfortable. But their tolls were high (few were ever profitable) and the poor often refrained from using them. Secondly, this meant that those unable or unwilling to pay the tolls did all they could to avoid passing through the toll-gates, often using their knowledge of long-forgotten by-roads to find an alternative to the turnpike. In turn this obliged the turnpike trusts to shut off or block many of these side roads, with the result that much of the old road network could no longer be used. Thirdly, and this must be regarded as the main contribution of the turnpike to social history, many of the turnpikes were laid out along new routes which altered and improved communications between the larger centres of population. A few incorporated short lengths of earlier roads but even today some of the best and most convenient roads in the county were once new turnpikes.

Although enclosure and road changes are the most widespread and easily recognizable factors in the desertion and shrinkage of villages neither can be regarded as the primary cause. Open fields and waste were not enclosed without reason and the subsequent desertion and shrinkage was, in most cases, inevitable. Similarly the pre-turnpike road system did not alter for no reason and its gradual changes took place in response to other events. Only in the case of the turnpikes themselves can road changes be considered as a direct cause of population movement, and so be regarded as the primary reason for desertion and shrinkage. What then are the principal influences that led to enclosure and the changes in the medieval road system?

There can be little doubt that the primary cause was numerical change in the population. For example, the enclosures of the eighteenth and nineteenth centuries were made more or less inevitable by an increasing population and the need to feed it. It was this rise in population which, more indirectly, provided the impetus for the introduction of the turnpikes. In earlier times however, particularly during the Middle Ages, the reverse was often true, especially in the aftermath of the Black Death.

The Black Death has already been mentioned and it is important to realize what an important effect it had. It was a form of bubonic plague which entered England, through the small Dorset port of Melcombe Regis, in the summer of 1348 and its results were devastating. It is generally estimated that the population of the country, then about 4 or 5 millions,[4] fell by from 30 to 50 per cent during the outbreak. There were also other outbreaks between 1350 and 1400 and some much later visitations were probably caused by the same form of disease.

It is not hard to imagine some of the innumerable consequences of this great reduction in population, a reduction which, it has been suggested, was not made good until about 1500. Yet what matters here is that the plague caused a shrinkage of arable land, not only because there were fewer to feed but because there were fewer to farm. As a result many of the old open fields were left uncultivated. This in turn led to newly surplus land being enclosed and used for purposes that required less human labour, such as sheep grazing. At the same time many of the smaller settlements merged to make better use of the remaining open fields. In short a proportion of the open field arable land and a certain number of small villages must have disappeared almost entirely, and it is surely no coincidence that the abandonment of many medieval villages has been attributed to the period between 1350 and 1500. The same applies to the existing communications system. Where communities disappeared so also did the roads that served them. But here it must be remembered that the effect was localized and had little effect on the complete network.

Other important influences in the decline of many rural communities were changes in local government (as it would now be called) and change of ownership or tenancy by sale or transfer. The former probably took the form of alterations to parish boundaries, but here research is made difficult by the lack of documentary evidence and by the fact that parish boundaries are not shown on any of the early small scale maps of the county. For in the days when the first maps were made the most important boundaries were those of the Hundreds and Liberties, land divisions which had existed since Saxon times and which were not finally abolished until County Councils were set up by the Local Government Acts of 1888 and 1889.

Some of the Saxon charters referred to in the text suggest that a few parishes, including some of the larger, have undergone little change, but the majority have probably suffered in one way or another, especially by the division of large parishes into several smaller ones. For instance the parish of Gillingham is thought to have covered 64,000 acres in the late eighteenth century and to have had a 40 mile boundary. The details of alterations to parishes have often been quoted in the text and it seems likely that many of them led to some reorientation of the local life and that in turn this was accompanied by a partial redistribution of the population. The parish of Hillfield provides an excellent example of this. In the latter part of the eighteenth century it was a chapelry in the parish of Sydling St Nicholas, in whose churchyard it buried its dead. As it stands on the southern edge of a section of the Blackmoor Vale where medieval communications were likely to have been poor, it looked more to the south than to the north, despite the physical obstacle of the great chalk scarp. Later, however, in the wake of the enclosure of commons and subsequent road improvements, it began to look north towards Sherborne, and it seems likely that its separation as a parish of its own is in some way connected with this change.

Owing to the intricacies of the feudal system change of ownership is another complex subject, but there are a few facts that can be stated. Many of the feudal lords or tenants-in-chief held estates made up of many scattered manors, most of which were occupied by sub-tenants, and any disturbance of this pattern (a common event throughout the Middle Ages) must have had repercussions at all levels on the social scale. Some manors may have acquired resident lords, others may have lost them, and both factors are likely to have caused some change in the distribution of population. It is also worth bearing in mind the cumulative effect on estates which became united by marriage, for this led to a change in geographical focus which often resulted in movement of labour.

Mention of marriage raises one of the most

fascinating aspects of medieval social history, namely the inheritance of land through heiresses. Time and again in Dorset the lack of male heirs led to estates being passed through the female line, and what were, in effect, mergers must have had some influence on the settlements on the estate. The subject of the status of the propertied spinster is outside the scope of this book but, prior to the Dissolution of the Monasteries, unmarried women had little choice other than marriage or the surrender of their property to the Church. Thus many of the largest estates in the county have been enlarged by union with estates inherited by heiresses whose subsequent marriage may have owed more to necessity than choice.

There are several additional factors that have caused the desertion and shrinkage of Dorset's villages and these may be best summed up in the words of the Litany: 'From lightning and tempest; from plague, pestilence and famine; from battle, murder and sudden death'. There was also fire, but, perhaps strangely, it seems unlikely that fire was a common cause of permanent population change. For one thing the medieval cottage was traditionally built of thatch, wattle and daub and was easily replaceable. Secondly, the character of the feudal system made movement from a manor or migration from one village to another all but impossible without the consent of the lord. Thirdly, society was much more closely integrated than it is today and personal local attachment would have had a strong influence against movement. Little is recorded of fires taking place in smaller communities other than Leland's remarks about Horton; the statement that Tarrant Rushton was apparently burnt down in the middle of the seventeenth century, and the probability that the vicarage and forty houses in Bere Regis were destroyed towards the end of the eighteenth century. Yet Dorset's towns were regularly swept by fire. Wareham in particular seems to have been ravaged by fire again and again, but there is no hint that there was ever any intention to abandon the site. Indeed, Wareham's location and the nature of its economy were such as to ensure reconstruction in the shortest possible time. Even in the case of Blandford, where the great fire of 1731 destroyed much of the town,

there is no mention of mass migration. Instead the inhabitants took the opportunity to rebuild the town in a style which is today regarded as a superb example of eighteenth-century architecture. Though these are towns, the same considerations are likely to have applied to Dorset's villages. It would therefore be unwise to attribute the disappearance of any particular settlement to fire unless there is strong supporting evidence.

The same comments apply to 'tempest', and the only authentic case of depopulation by storm is that of East Fleet where, in 1824, part of the old village was destroyed by the sea during a gale. This however took place comparatively recently and the unhoused were probably easily accommodated nearby. There is no record of a similar event taking place inland. Exceptionally heavy and prolonged rain may have caused local landslips from time to time, such as occurred in the sixteenth century when part of the north face of High Stoy collapsed, and the 1 inch maps of the Geological Survey (Sheets 312 and 327) show considerable areas of what they call 'landslip' round the western edge of the Chalk, particularly in the Powerstock Vales, but since both Askwerswell and Chilcombe and several ancient farmsteads stand on the largest of these areas, these landslips must have taken place long ago.

Of the next three – 'plague, pestilence and famine' – there is little to say about the last except to note that Dorset is unlikely to have been immune to its effects. The pillaging that took place after the Norman Conquest, during which it is thought that half of Dorchester's houses were sacked, and the lawlessness of the following century must inevitably have caused local food shortages. But Dorset's wide range of agricultural soils are likely to have saved its populace from the worst effects of famine; and in any case unorganized human movement was almost impossible within the practical limitations of medieval life, nor did it offer a satisfactory remedy for famine.

Pestilence and plague have played an important role in the history of Dorset's villages, because not only could they be, in themselves, a major cause of depopulation but they could, and did, result in the long-term or even permanent abandonment of sites. It seems that the plague and its variants were endemic in this country from Saxon times until the end of the seventeenth century. Though the Black Death was by far the most serious of these epidemics, most of these outbreaks went unrecorded and it is not until the latter half of the seventeenth century that direct evidence of its occurrence in rural areas is to be found. There are two notable examples of the destructive effects of the plague in Dorset, namely at Lytchett Matravers and Mapperton. The former strengthens the belief that sites once devastated by plague were avoided for many decades after the disease had passed by; for the settlement at Lytchett was never rebuilt on the original site, and the present village is of much later date. It is tempting to attribute other known desertions to the effects of the plague, but this leads all too easily into the realm of unsupportable speculation. Nevertheless it is worth making the tentative suggestion that the complete abandonment of Colber may have been caused by the plague. It would have been natural in such circumstances for Sturminster Newton to isolate itself from the danger of infection, and this in part explains the severing of the natural route between the two across the River Stour. The abandonment of Knowlton also hints at the possibilities of plague, and here there is the additional ingredient of a prehistoric, and therefore pagan, background which may have produced something like a taboo on the site. Perhaps the church alone was allowed to remain because it was consecrated? Plague is also mentioned as a factor in the decline of Radipole.

It would be idle to claim that Dorset has not had its fair share of 'murder and sudden death', but these can be dismissed as causes of depopulation or human migration on any scale. As to 'battle', Dorset has been fortunate in that since Saxon times it has never been the scene of any major land conflict. The county only played a minor part in the Wars of the Roses and was not the arena for any of the more savage or less picturesque episodes in the Civil Wars, and it seems that these struggles had little effect on the population. This internal tranquillity is reflected in the fact that most of the places mentioned in Domesday Book had already been

settled for many centuries and that, as far as identification is possible, all of these are still known today, either by site, by name, or by both.

There are, it is true, two places where human violence is claimed to have been the cause of destruction, West Ringstead and West Bexington, and though in neither case is the evidence very convincing their abandonment has been attributed to foreign raiders. In the former the tradition is weak and historians have paid little attention to it; in the latter the tradition is stronger and Hutchins gives a circumstantial account of it. But the part of the coast concerned is not propitious for such a raid, and medieval West Bexington can hardly have been an obvious source of worthwhile ransom. A more mundane explanation for the village's decline is that it was destroyed by a storm, but even this is unlikely if the old settlement occupied a site as high above sea level as West Bexington Farm. Perhaps after all the story of the raid is credible.

Such then is a summary of the factors which emerge most clearly as having contributed to the disappearance and shrinkage of villages in Dorset since late Saxon times. The impact of these factors suggest that Dorset is not a county which has known great change in the distribution of its population, and the abiding impression is one of continuity of settlement. One reason for this is probably closely connected with the history of the county between the breakdown of the Roman administration and the Norman Conquest, for it seems to have been able to absorb the arrival of the Saxons without suffering the disturbance that marked their arrival in other parts of the south and east.

Though it is almost impossible to make any broader generalizations, there does seem to be a kind of sequence in the history of settlement in Dorset that may be of wider significance. During the Middle Ages change seems to have centred on the integration and consolidation of villages – a process in which some of the smaller and weaker disappeared; but during the sixteenth, seventeenth and eighteenth centuries, when most of the enclosures took place, the process seems to have been reversed, and part of the rural population spread out from the villages into the many farmsteads and farms that gradually developed during these centuries. It is interesting to note that the same thing has happened in more recent times, though on a much smaller scale and for different reasons. In the mid-nineteenth century the population of Dorset's villages stood at its highest, but from then on until 1914 the agricultural depression led to a steady migration, not to outlying farms, but to the towns. Once again the process has been reversed, because the arrival of the motor car has reduced distance, and Dorset's villages, even its farms, have been revived by an influx of people who live in one place and work in another. But this has altered the immemorial pattern of village life much less than might have been expected. It has inevitably brought change, but the change has been evolutionary rather then revolutionary, and it has done little to alter the age-old features of a county some of whose villages, hamlets, farmsteads and farms have probably known human occupation ever since the first settlers reached these shores.

Notes

CHAPTER 1

[1] Almack, A. C., Proc. 38 1917.
[2] Chancellor, E. C., Proc. 56 1934.
[3] Good, R., *A Geographical Handbook of the Dorset Flora* 1948.
[4] Fletcher, J. M. J., Proc. 43 1922.
[5] Grundy, G. B., Proc. 57 1935 *et seq.*
[6] Drew, C. D., Proc. 69 1947.
[7] Finburg, H. P. R., *The Early Charters of Wessex* (1964).
[8] Pope, A., Proc. 30 1909.
[9] Sellman, R. R., *Illustrations of Dorset History* (1960).
[10] Dicker, C. H. W., Proc. 30 1909.

CHAPTER 2

[1] Oswald A. *Country Life*, 26th July 1962.

CHAPTER 3

[1] Baker, Sir T., Proc. 17 1896.
[2] Taylor, C. C., *Dorset* (1970).
[3] Cantor, L. M. and Wilson, J. D., Proc. 90 1968.
[4] Drew, C. D., Proc. 69 1947.
[5] Taylor, C. C., Proc. 88 1967.
[6] Drew, C. D., Proc. 78 1956.
[7] Barrett, A., *The Dorset Year Book*, 1975–75.
[8] Rahtz, P. A., Proc. 81 1959.
[9] Bailey, C. J., Proc. 87 1965.
[10] *Ibid.*, Proc. 95 1973.
[11] Hine, R., *History of Beaminster* (Taunton, 1914).
[12] Bartelot, R. G., Proc. 66 1944.

CHAPTER 4

[1] For the history of Milton Abbas see Fookes, C. H. R., *Milton Abbas, Dorset* (n.d.).
[2] Wansborough, R., *The Tale of Milton Abbas* (Milborne Port, 1974).
[3] Farrar, R. A. H., Proc. 97 1975.
[4] Fletcher, W. J., Proc. 28 1907.
[5] See Bankes, W. R., Proc. 11 1890, and Bankes, V., *A Dorset Heritage* (1953).
[6] Fletcher, J. M. J., Proc. 39 1918.
[7] Pentin, H., Proc. 36 1915.
[8] See the excellent guide to Smedmore and Kimmeridge by J. C. Mansel.
[9] Eastwood, F. B., Proc. 49 1928.

CHAPTER 5

[1] Sykes, E. R., Proc. 59 1937.
[2] Pentin, H., Proc. 30 1909.
[3] Drew, C. D., Proc. 69 1947.
[4] *RCHM* and Eyton, R. W., *A Key to Domesday* (Dorchester, 1878).
[5] Hutchins, J., 1st edition, Vol. II, p. 492 and elsewhere.
  Bath, M., Proc. 95 1973.
[6] Fowler, J., *Medieval Sherborne* (Dorchester, 1951).
[7] Batten, J., Proc. 9 1888.
  Bartelot, R. G., Proc. 66 1944.
[8] Bailey, C. J., *in litt.*
[9] Bailey, C. J., *Somerset & Dorset Notes & Queries.* XXX 1971.
  Bailey, C. J., Proc. 95 1973.
[10] Cantor, L. M. and Wilson, J. D., Proc. 85 1963.
[11] Hardy, W. M., *Old Swanage and Purbeck* (Dorchester, 1910).
[12] Filliter, W. D., Proc. 22 1901.
[13] Bond, Mrs. Ivo, *Tyneham*, Dorchester, 1956.
[14] Dru Drury, G., Proc. 70 1948.
[15] Legg, R., *Purbeck Island* (Milborne Port, 1972).

CHAPTER 6

[1] See *VCH* Vol. II (1908).
[2] Dru Drury, G., Proc. 64 1943.
[3] Dayrell-Reed, T., Proc. 53 1931.
[4] Wellington, G., Proc. 17 1896.
  Dru Drury, G., Proc. 51 1929.
[5] Fletcher, J. M. J., Proc. 49 1928.
[6] For a plan see *RCHM* Vol. III.
[7] For an account of the manor house and barn see Oswald, A., *Country Life*, 2 August 1962.
[8] Hutchins, J., Vol. I, p. 437.
[9] Maturin, M. P., Proc. 43 1922.
  Pope, A., Proc. 45 1924.
[10] Grundy, G. B., Proc. 59 1937.
[11] For an illustration see *RCHM* Vol. IV.
[12] Ouvry, J. D., Proc. 49 1928.
[13] For an excellent description and map see *RCHM*, Vol. III.
[14] *ORD*, p. 135.
[15] Sanderson, A., *Trent in Dorset* (Dorchester, 1969).
[16] For evidence that burial was also denied the people of Mapperton in 1582 see Barrington, N., *Dorset* No. 46 1975.

[17] For an account of the disaster see Barnes, W. M., Proc. 19 1897.

[18] Good, R., *Weyland* p. 29.

[19] See parish registers quoted by Hutchins in ed. 1, Vol. II, p. 416.

CHAPTER 7

[1] Hutchins, J., 1st ed., Vol. I p. 421.

[2] Taylor, C. C., 'Lost Dorset Place Names' Proc. 89 1967.

[3] Robinson, Sir J. C., Proc. 18 1897.

[4] Taylor, C. C., *op. cit.*

[5] *Ibid.*

[6] Bailey, C. J. (*in litt*).

[7] For evidence of this see line 9, column 2, page 94 of Hutchins' 1st edition where the comma may be misplaced.

[8] Almack, T. F., *Village Heritage* (Dorchester 1961). Drew, C. D., Proc. 71 1949.

[9] Dru Drury, G., Proc. 54 1932. *Ibid.*, Proc. 55 1933.

[10] Taylor, C. C., *op. cit.*

[11] *Ibid.*

[12] Hutchins, J., 1st edn., Vol. I, p. 143.

[13] Dayrell-Reed, T., Proc. 53 1931.

[14] Drawn by C. D. Drew and now in the Library of the County Museum, Dorchester.

[15] Drew, C. D., Proc. 64 1942. *ORD*, p. 57.

[16] Dayrell-Reed, T., Proc. 53 1931.

[17] Grundy, G. B., Proc. 58 1936.

[18] Taylor, C. C., *op. cit.*

[19] For an account of the project see Sellman, R. R. *Illustrations of Dorset History*, London 1960.

[20] Taylor, C. C., *op. cit.*

[21] Cantor, L. M. and Wilson, J. D., Proc. 86, 1964.

[22] Fägersten, A., *Dorset Place Names*, Uppsala, 1933.

[23] Best, W. S., *Somerset & Dorset Notes & Queries*, XXVII 1961.

[24] Taylor, C. C., *op. cit.*

[25] *Ibid.*

[26] For further information see Taylor, C. C., *op. cit.*,

CHAPTER 8

[1] Bettey, J. H., Proc. 97 1975.

[2] Roscoe, E. (ed.), *The Marnh'll Book* (Gillingham, 1952).

[3] For a detailed examination of the turnpike system see *ORD*.

[4] Gasquet, F. A., *The Great Pestilence* (London, 1883).

Index

Places and place-names mentioned only incidentally in the text
are not included. The spelling follows that of 1 OS 1970.